Ebby:
THE MAN WHO SPONSORED BILL W.

Bill Wilson (left) and Ebby at the Second International Convention of AA in St. Louis in 1955.

Ebby:

THE MAN WHO
SPONSORED BILL W.

Mel B.

[Ebby] pushed ajar that great gate
through which all in AA have since passed
to find their freedom under God.

Bill W.
In his remembrance of Ebby,
AA Grapevine, June 1966

Hazelden
Publishing

Hazelden Publishing
Center City, Minnesota 55012-0176
hazelden.org/bookstore

©1998 by Hazelden Foundation
All rights reserved. Published 1998
Printed in the United States of America
No portion of this publication may be reproduced in any
manner without the written permission of the publisher

ISBN: 978-1-56838-162-6

Book design by Will H. Powers
Typesetting by Stanton Publication Services, Inc.

Quotations from literature published by
Alcoholics Anonymous World Services, Inc.
are reprinted by permission of A.A. World Services, Inc.

In gratitude to

William P. Harris
Lynchburg, Virginia

Dr. Vernon O. Ray
Rockford, Illinois

*who donated funds for
the production of this book.*

Contents

Foreword

The year was 1934. Newly elected President Franklin D. Roosevelt, with the United States in the turmoil of the Great Depression, declared, "The only thing we have to fear is fear itself." National Prohibition ended. The movie *King Kong* was playing at Radio City Music Hall to sellout crowds. Admission was ten cents. For those who were working, the average household income was $1,048. Outside Chicago's Biograph Theater, a barrage of FBI bullets brought down Public Enemy No. 1, John Dillinger. Bob Hope's radio show premiered. In New York City a sober Ebby Thacher made a phone call to his old friend and drinking buddy, a drunken Bill Wilson. Ebby's phone call set in motion a series of events that have changed, for the better, the lives of millions of men and women and their families the world over.

The biography that follows highlights the message of recovery Ebby presented to Bill and the subsequent founding and growth of the fellowship and program of Alcoholics Anonymous. One may ask, why a biography of Ebby? After all, it is well known in the AA fellowship that Ebby's only significant role in AA was to carry the message of hope to Bill. He had little to do with the writing of the Big Book or the laborious work of getting the early AA society established and functioning. Later on, he even became a sort of hanger-on who seemed to trade on his friendship with Bill.

His life followed a pattern that is all too familiar in many AA groups: early sobriety and periods of recovery interrupted by repeated slips. So why should we be interested in such an individual, whose grasp of the AA program appears weak and whose practice of it couldn't be singled out as a shining example? And why would Bill call Ebby his sponsor for twenty-two years?

AA members and friends can benefit by studying AA's roots and the process and people who brought the movement into being. Rightly and deservedly, we all acknowledge the splendid contributions of AA's cofounders, Bill Wilson and Dr. Bob Smith and their wives, Lois and Anne. But these founders did not create the fellowship out of nothing, and they had the support and cooperation of many other people both in and out of AA. Ebby Thacher was one of these key people.

There are at least five reasons for reviewing Ebby's life and his relationship to AA.

Honesty should be the first reason for looking at Ebby's life. AA is described as an honest program, but there have been times when misleading or insufficient information has been presented as fact in AA history. Until recently, for example, there was an effort to downplay the role of the Oxford Group, the fellowship that supplied most of AA's spiritual principles. Such exclusions were supposedly for a good purpose. But this implies that truth could be damaging to AA. This is a strange position, as AA members are urged to face the truth fearlessly in their own lives. Why should truth be good for individual members but not for the fellowship?

Gratitude is a second reason for reviewing Ebby's life. It is to Bill W's credit that he never lost his gratitude to Ebby, despite Ebby's often woeful and irresponsible behavior. This is a good lesson for AA members, who sometimes become too critical of sponsors and members who return to drinking.

Knowledge is a third reason for gaining more understanding of Ebby. It is generally agreed that learning from the past, without living in it, is healthy. At a critical time in AA's birthing period, Ebby received excellent sponsorship from Oxford Group members and then carried that message in the right way to the person who was obviously qualified to carry it to the world. Though much has been learned since then, there has been little change in this basic idea: People help themselves by trying to help others, and this is the process that helps alcoholics get sober and stay that way.

Love and tolerance of others, as stated on page 84 of the text of Alcoholics Anonymous, is the "code" of living that is suggested to AA members. Those in recovery make progress by learning to practice love and tolerance for themselves and especially for other people. Bill W. certainly showed love and tolerance toward Ebby, who some refer to as "AA's Troubled Messenger." While reading the life story of Ebby, some may want to consider: *Love and tolerance of others* is our code.

A final reason for studying Ebby's life is that many AA members and friends of the fellowship have an insatiable curiosity about Ebby and his destiny. This curiosity led the author, Mel B., to learn more about Ebby and to share it with his readers. Mel is qualified for this undertaking. Mel is now in his forty-eighth year as a member of AA, author of many pamphlets and books (including contributions to AA's book *Pass It On*), friend of the late Bill Wilson, and gifted speaker. Also, to Mel's credit is his unselfish mentoring of many authors, archivists, and students of AA's history.

Mel's wish for this book is that it will add knowledge and understanding, not only about Ebby, but also for those individuals whose lives are helped by AA but who may not be "perfect" members throughout their lives. Mel has written this book for those interested in AA's history, but primarily it is written for individuals in the fellowship today and others who will join AA in the future. We should all commend Mel for this wonderful undertaking.

BILL PITTMAN
Administrator, Hazelden Archives/HP Archives Press

A Note On Anonymity

In this biography, I have taken care to protect the anonymity of all persons identified as AA members. The exception is Ebby; in his case, I have followed the precedent of using full last names that was established by AA World Services in its own two biographies of the AA co-founders. And as noted in Bill Wilson's biography *Pass It On,* the AA Twelve Traditions make no reference to *posthumous* anonymity.

Although no AA Tradition governs anonymity after death, a developing custom is to respect the wishes of the surviving family members. Ebby's closest living relatives, a niece and a nephew, endorsed this project and gave me permission to use Ebby's surname in the text. I hope readers will agree that what I've described above meets reasonable requirements for full disclosure of a deceased AA member's last name.

Photo Credits

Photo	Credit
Frontispiece, Bill W. and Ebby in St. Louis	Photograph from AA Archives
Page 4, Ebby as young man	Photograph supplied by Ellen FitzPatrick
Page 26, Thacher home	Photograph supplied by Melanie Otis
Page 28, Ebby with fish	Photograph supplied by Ellen FitzPatrick
Page 136, Margaret and Mickey McPike with Bill W.	Photograph supplied by Margaret Donohue
Page 140, The McPike farmhouse	Photograph supplied by Margaret Donohue
Page 148, Ebby in his final months	Photograph supplied by Margaret Donohue

Acknowledgments

The idea for a book about Ebby Thacher came from Thomas B., a professional counselor from Islip, New York, and Margaret McPike, the woman who cared for Ebby during the last two years of this life. Margaret, who died in 1982, granted me a useful interview and a tour of McPike's Farm, while Thomas turned over his notes to me when it became clear that his busy practice wouldn't give him time to write the story.

Melanie Otis and her mother, Nancy Otis, gave me useful information about Manchester, Vermont. Others I wish to acknowledge include Frank M. and Judit Santon of the AA Archives, Searcy W. (Ebby's Texas sponsor), Ellen FitzPatrick (Ebby's niece), the late Ken Thacher, Jr. (Ebby's nephew), Robert Olcott, Nell Wing, Willard Hunter, Jan Van Shoubrouek, George Trotter, Jim Blair, and Bill White. Lyn H., a graduate student at Vanderbilt, supplied letters from High Watch, while Jennifer Hamburg did important typing. Margaret McPike's daughter, Margaret Donohue, was very helpful in providing information about Ebby's stay at McPike's Farm. I also relied on information obtained from Lib S. and Eve M., longtime AA members who worked at the General Service Office in New York. Others, now deceased, who supplied useful facts were Lois Wilson, Marty M., and Shep C.

ACKNOWLEDGMENTS

I am grateful for help from these generous friends. Any mistakes in this story, of course, are my own.

The publisher gratefully acknowledges the following who reviewed the manuscript and added helpful suggestions: Margaret R. Graves, Louis F. Hill, Damian McElrath, Ph.D., and William Cope Moyers.

Ebby:
THE MAN WHO SPONSORED BILL W.

1

A Call from an Old Friend

Late November 1934 seemed to be the worst of times for Bill Wilson, an unemployed and completely discredited stock-broker living in Brooklyn, New York. He had fallen from a lofty place in life. Less than six years earlier, everything had been going his way: a luxury apartment, fat profits in a booming stock market, expensive vacations in resort areas, and a host of superficial Wall Street friends who, as he later recalled, "spent in thousands and chattered in millions."

But something else in Bill's world had been soaring with the stock market—a savage drinking problem that was already well out of control even before the Great Crash of 1929 left him shocked and virtually penniless. From 1929 to 1934, drinking destroyed two promising chances of a business comeback. Twice hospitalized for alcoholism, he was now a broken man, totally dependent on his wife's meager earnings as a department-store clerk, and fearful that he would soon have to be locked up forever.

Then he received a telephone call from an old friend—a call that would change his life and, through an amazing chain process, the lives of millions of others who would eventually follow Bill into sobriety in Alcoholics Anonymous, a fellowship that reveres him today as its cofounder.

The caller was Ebby Thacher, a friend from Bill's childhood

3

Ebby as a young man.

years. Ebby had joined Bill for a drunken airplane ride in January 1929—a crazy experience in those early days of aviation that could have been the end for both of them. The years since that frightful event had been bad for Ebby too. Bill had even heard that his old friend might be headed for an insane asylum. But on this day, Ebby was in nearby Manhattan and wanted to see him. Bill, well into days of drinking, immediately invited him over in the hope they could drink together. "Unmindful of his welfare," Bill later recalled, "I thought only of recapturing the spirit of other days."

But Ebby had not come to drink. Now sober after years of destructive drinking, he had come to carry a message. A few months earlier, in Bennington, Vermont, three men had intervened while he stood before a judge, expecting stiff punishment for yet another drunken episode. The men were members of the Oxford Group, an evangelical movement then having great success in helping troubled people. Their spiritual program had restored Ebby to sobriety; now he wanted to pass the same message on to his old friend Bill.

Ebby's call couldn't have been timed more perfectly. Since 1933, Bill had been making desperate efforts to stop drinking, but nothing had worked. He was an intelligent, capable man who prided himself on his ability to fight his way through most problems, but none of this had worked with his drinking. Facing complete collapse, he was open to any suggestion that offered even slight hope.

Bill, speaking nearly ten years later in New Haven at the Yale Summer School of Alcohol Studies, recalled Ebby's arrival as the very day that Alcoholics Anonymous commenced to take shape. But he was not sure at the time that he wanted Ebby's message. "I remember his coming into my kitchen, where I was half-drunk," Bill told the Yale summer students.

5

I was afraid that perhaps he had come to reform me. You know, curiously enough, we alcoholics are very sensitive on this subject of reform. I could not quite make out my friend. I could see something different about him but I could not put my finger on it. So finally I said, "Ebby, what's got into you?" And he said, "Well, I've got religion." That shocked me terribly, for I was one of those people with a dandy modern education which had taught me that self-sufficiency would be enough to carry me through life, and here was a man talking a point of view which collided with mine.

According to Bill, Ebby then explained how the Oxford Group members had offered him a program involving personal moral inventory, admission to another person of wrongs done, making amends and restitution, and an effort to be of real service to others. Beyond that, the Oxford Groupers had also suggested that Ebby needed to call on God, as he understood God, to help Ebby with his problem. It was apparently working, for he had been sober now for two months.

These were the ideas that Bill would later formulate as the Twelve Steps of Alcoholics Anonymous. But on that November day, he was barely able to consider them. He also found himself resisting the suggestion that he should try prayer. But again and again in later years, he would acknowledge how skillfully Ebby presented the message to him. He did it in such a way that Bill would at least consider it. "You see, here was my friend talking to me, one alcoholic talking to another," Bill explained to the Yale group. "I could no longer say, 'He doesn't understand me.' Sure he understood me. We had done a lot of drinking together, and gone the same route of humiliation, despair, and defeat. Yes, he could understand."

Ebby went back to where he was living, a rescue mission in Manhattan operated by Calvary Episcopal Church. Bill continued to drink, but his old friend's example had left a deep impression. "The good of what he said stuck so well that in no waking moment thereafter could I get that man and his message out of my head," Bill recalled many years later. And when Bill's wife, Lois, came home, they talked about it. "At times I felt rather excited and both of us began to use a word we had forgotten. That word was 'hope.' However, I kept on drinking, but now more restrained."

Ebby's next move was to arrive one afternoon with Shep C., one of the three men who had intervened for him with the judge in Vermont. Though Bill had known Shep C. in Manchester, Vermont, since 1919, he didn't like what Shep had to say. "He gave me the Oxford Group's boast, aggressively and with all the punch he could pack," Bill remembered. "I didn't like this at all. When they were gone I took to the bottle and really punished it. But the mood swings went on, rebellion to hope and back again."

In a maudlin state one day, Bill decided to visit Calvary Mission, where Ebby was staying. "I figured I'd go and see what did they do, anyway, down there. I'd find out."

Calvary Mission was at 246 East Twenty-Third Street, near the southwest corner of Second Avenue. This rescue mission was operated by the Episcopalian Calvary Church, whose pastor, Dr. Sam Shoemaker, had an important role in the Oxford Group and who would become a mentor to Bill. In operation from 1926 to 1936, the mission aided thousands of homeless men like Ebby, offering them lodging, two meals a day, and a spiritual message of hope. It had a crucial role in bringing Ebby and Bill together at this critical time. It's doubtful that Ebby would have even been living in New York City without the mission.

But it took Bill most of a day to reach the mission. After leaving the subway at Fourth Avenue and Twenty-Third Street in lower Manhattan, he visited a number of bars before arriving at the mission around nightfall. Accompanied by a Finnish fisherman named Alec, he was in terrible condition. Tex Francisco, the ex-drunk who was in charge, even proposed to run them out. But Ebby turned up and invited both of them to a plate of beans. Then he suggested they attend a meeting in the mission. Bill said:

> The three of us were soon sitting on one of the hard wooden benches that filled the place. I shivered a little as I looked at the derelict audience. I could smell sweat and alcohol. What the suffering was, I pretty well knew.
>
> There were hymns and prayers. Tex, the leader, exhorted us. Only Jesus could save, he said. Certain men got up and made testimonials. Numb as I was, I felt interest and excitement rising. Then came the call [to repent our sins]. Penitents started marching forward to the rail. Unaccountably impelled, I started too, dragging Alec with me. Ebby reached for my coattails, but it was too late.
>
> Soon, I knelt among the sweating, stinking penitents. Maybe then and there, for the very first time, I was penitent, too. Something touched me. I guess it was more than that. I was hit. I felt a wild impulse to talk. Jumping to my feet, I began.

Bill, even though drunk, apparently managed to make himself understood. "Afterward, I could never remember what I said," he noted in 1954. "I only knew that I was in earnest and people seemed to pay attention. Afterward, Ebby, who had been scared to death, told me with relief that I had done all right and had given my heart to God."

But Bill's surrender was not yet complete, although the experience in the mission had a profound effect on him. Returning home, he had a long, hopeful talk with Lois and actually had a good night's sleep. He had a terrible hangover the next day, however, and took a few drinks to "cure" it. This was his undoing, and he drank on for another two or three days. Still, he kept pondering the mission experience. He began to view his alcoholic condition in the same way a cancer patient might regard that illness. Later, he would say:

> But alcoholism is my illness, not cancer. Yet what was the difference? Was not alcoholism also a consumer of body and mind? And, perhaps, if one had such a thing, of soul? Alcoholism took longer to kill, but the result was the same. Yes, if there was any great physician that could cure the alcohol sickness, I'd better find him now, at once. I'd better find what my friend had found. Was I like the cancer sufferer who would do anything to get well? If getting well required me to pray at high noon in the public square with other sufferers, would I swallow my pride and do that? Maybe I would.

This state of mind, which today's AA members might recognize as that of a person approaching complete defeat, led Bill to return to New York's Charles B. Towns Hospital. He had been treated there earlier by an unusual doctor named William D. Silkworth. Dr. Silkworth had considered Bill an excellent prospect for recovery because of his high intelligence, strong determination, and seeming ability to comprehend the facts about his problem. Though Bill's subsequent drinking had disappointed Silkworth, the doctor still had great affection for him. Bill, still drinking and waving a bottle, arrived back at Towns Hospital on December 11, 1934. Dr. Silkworth immediately sent him to a room.

During the next few days, Dr. Silkworth put Bill through a detoxification process that included barbiturates, doses of bella donna, and a little sedative. "I wasn't in such bad shape this time," Bill said, "for it would have taken me another sixty days of hard drinking to bring me to the verge of delirium tremens. So I began to clear up quite rapidly. But the clearer I got, the more my spirits fell. I began to be frightfully depressed and Lois came to see me each night after work, looking so sad and sick. The depression would become appalling after she left." He began to think that it would be a good thing if he were to die.

Then Ebby returned on the morning of December 14. Bill remembered him as looking the picture of health and confidence. "Mighty sorry you had to land up here again," Ebby said. "Thought I'd come up and say 'hello.'" Bill later remembered feeling better as Ebby started to talk. "What he said at this point I don't remember, but I did notice that he pointedly avoided the topics of alcohol and religion. He was just paying a friendly visit, asking for nothing. He wasn't going to try any evangelism on me after all."

Since Ebby didn't bring up these subjects, Bill did. And Ebby then went over the points he had made during his first visit at Bill's home. "Again he told how he found he couldn't run his own life," Bill said, "how he got honest with himself as never before. How he'd been making amends to the people he'd damaged. How he'd been trying to give of himself without putting a price tag on his efforts, and finally how he'd tried prayer just as an experiment and had found to his surprise that it worked." Bill recalled:

> Once more he emphasized the difference between being on the water wagon and his present state. He no longer had to fight the desire to drink. The desire had been lifted right out of him. It had simply vanished. He no longer sat on a powder keg. He was released. He was free. That was his simple story.

Ebby, after explaining this to Bill, promised to return soon and left the hospital. After he'd gone, the temporary lift Bill had received from the visit disappeared, and he found himself having mental arguments with what he'd heard. His depression deepened and, as he remembered it, the "terrifying darkness had become complete. In agony of spirit, I again thought of the cancer of alcoholism that had now consumed me in mind and spirit, and soon the body. . . . For a brief moment, I suppose, the last trace of my obstinacy was crushed out as the abyss yawned."

Bill, without realizing it, had reached a point that he would later describe as ego deflation at depth. "I remember saying to myself, 'I'll do anything, anything at all! If there be a Great Physician, I'll call on him.' Then, with neither faith nor hope I cried out, 'If there be a God, let Him show Himself.' "

What then followed was an astonishing experience that would someday be tagged in Alcoholics Anonymous as Bill's "Hot Flash." It would be described briefly in the opening chapter of "Bill's Story" in the basic text, *Alcoholics Anonymous,*

About six months later, a business trip would take Bill to Akron, Ohio, where he would meet another alcoholic named Dr. Bob Smith. The two of them would become cofounders of Alcoholics Anonymous. In time, Bill would be honored by thousands of recovering alcoholics who would rise as one person when he stepped onto an auditorium stage. Yale University would offer him an honorary doctorate, and *Time* magazine would seek to feature him on its cover. He would decline such honors. But at his passing in January 1971, the *New York Times* and other newspapers around the country would give his obituary front-page treatment.

---

when it was first published in 1939. In 1954, Bill would furnish this longer version in his taped memories. Here's how this appears as it was published in 1984 in his biography, *Pass It On:*

> What happened next was electric. Suddenly, my room blazed with an indescribably white light. I was seized with an ecstasy beyond description. Every joy I had known was pale by comparison. The light, the ecstasy—I was conscious of nothing else for a time.
>
> Then, seen in the mind's eye, there was a mountain. I stood upon its summit, where a great wind blew. A wind, not of air; but of spirit. In great, clean strength, it blew right through me. Then came the blazing thought, "You are a free man." I know not at all how long I remained in this state, but finally the light and the ecstasy subsided. I again saw the wall of my room. As I became more quiet, a great peace stole over me, and this was accompanied by a sensation difficult to describe. I became acutely conscious of a Presence which seemed like a veritable sea of living spirit. I lay on the shores of a new world. "This," I thought, "must be the great reality. The God of the preachers."
>
> Savoring my new world, I remained in this state for a long time. I seemed to be possessed by the absolute, and the curious conviction deepened that no matter how wrong things seemed to be, there could be no question of the ultimate rightness of God's universe. For the first time, I felt that I really belonged. I knew that I was loved and could love in return. I thanked my God, who had given me a glimpse of His absolute self. Even though a pilgrim upon an uncertain highway, I need be concerned no more, for I had glimpsed the great beyond.

This experience, which was like "the lightning that comes out of the east and shines into the west," was something Bill would never have again with such intensity. But it marked a major turning point for him. At thirty-nine, he still had a long life ahead of him, a life that would have its peaks and valleys. But his life would still place him, as *Life* magazine did in 1990, among the most influential Americans of the twentieth century. He would leave Towns Hospital as a recovering alcoholic now zealously dedicated to the mission of helping other alcoholics.

And what about Ebby Thacher, the man who had carried the Oxford Group message to Bill with such care and devotion? What would happen to him? How would people respond to him as a person who had been a vital link in AA's founding? How did his friends remember him after his death in 1966?

That's a story worth telling. Bill and Ebby would be friends for the rest of their lives, as they were when they took that daring airplane ride in 1929. The future would largely be a splendid flight for Bill. But for Ebby, there would be times when he would all but crash and burn.

2

Friends from Different Worlds

Ebby Thacher and Bill Wilson both grew up in the early part of the 1900s in the eastern United States. They first knew each other as teenagers in Manchester, Vermont. Bill was only five months older than Ebby, and for a year they were in high school together. But their family circumstances were hardly similar.

Bill, born in East Dorset, Vermont, on November 26, 1895, grew up under ordinary circumstances, although he was never deprived in a material sense. East Dorset is only seven miles north of Manchester, a lovely resort town, where well-to-do families like Ebby's family were known as "summer people." Though Bill's maternal grandfather, Fayette Griffith, was a successful small-businessman who doted on his precocious grandson, Bill implied that the Thachers were much higher on the social scale than his own family. The Griffiths were substantial people, however. One of Fayette's cousins even became Vermont's first millionaire, according to Lois Wilson. Bill was always proud of his heritage through the Griffith line of relatives—and proud that his family included judges, lawyers, and other professionals and businesspeople of prominence in the state.

The Thachers, on the other hand, were a business and political dynasty with family roots going back to England and

15

seventeenth-century colonial America. In England, the family even had a coat of arms. The Thachers arrived in America in 1635. Their first American ancestor was said to be the Reverend Thomas Thacher, the first pastor of the old South Church in Boston. (There is even a Thacher Street in the heart of that city.) Thomas's father was the Reverend Peter Thacher, rector of St. Edmunds church in Wiltshire, England. Thomas's grandfather was the Reverend Peter Thacher, vicar of the parish of Queen Camel, in Somersetshire, England. There were actually five generations of clergy in the Thacher line. According to official New York history, these were accompanied by an equal number of distinguished laypersons, eminent in law, business, the military, literature, and politics.

Captain Samuel Thacher is believed to have commanded a company in 1750 during the French and Indian War. The Thacher name also appears on military rolls during the American Revolution. A Dr. James Thacher was a surgeon who also authored a history of medical events during the American Revolution and served as a medical officer during the war.

Dr. James Thacher noted that at least a thousand wounded were brought from the battlefields during the Revolutionary War and treated at the Albany hospital. "We have 30 surgeons, and all are constantly employed," he wrote. "The wounded of the British and Hessian troops are accommodated in the same hospital with our own, and receive equal attention.

"The foreigners are under the care of their own surgeons. I have been present at several of their capital operations and remember that the English surgeons perform with skill and dexterity; but the Germans, with few exceptions, do no credit to their profession."

The founder of the family fortune was Ebby's grandfather, George H. Thacher (1818–87). George came to Albany in 1849 and entered the railroad car wheel business in 1852. With the railroads about to become the major transportation industry, this was the ideal time to become a parts manufacturer of railroad equipment. The company became a principal supplier of wheels for the New York Central Railroad.

The company continued to grow under the leadership of Ebby's father, George H. Thacher, Jr. (1851–1929), and his uncle, John Boyd Thacher (1847–1909). Their company, the Thacher Car Wheel Works, became known as George H. Thacher & Company until 1919, when it was incorporated as the Thacher Propeller and Foundry Company.

Starting with Ebby's grandfather George Thacher, the family became attached to the Democratic Party and apparently never wavered. George was elected Albany's mayor in 1860, on the eve of the Civil War.

According to an Albany historian, the following year opened with the state's antislavery convention, held in Albany when other cities had denied the abolitionists their rights to peaceful assembly and free speech. Some groups in Albany urged Mayor Thacher to deny the city's hospitality to the abolitionists, but George replied with an emphatic negative:

> Let at least the Capital of the Empire State be kept free from the disgraceful proceedings which, in other localities, have brought dishonor upon our institutions. At all events, come what may, mob rule shall never prevail in our good city with my consent and connivance.

It's doubtful that, as a Democrat, Mayor Thacher would have supported Abraham Lincoln's 1860 election. Still he pulled out all the stops to provide a warm welcome when Lincoln visited

Albany on his way to take office in Washington. It was a dramatic journey for Lincoln, facing Southern secession and the threat of war. In *O Albany!* William Kennedy described the scene on the afternoon of February 18, 1861. The president-elect arrived in Albany in a train, "pulled by a highly polished locomotive bearing the name *Erastus Corning, Jr.* [after the son of Albany's premier businessman, Erastus Corning, president of the New York Central Railroad]. As the train passed the Central's West Albany shops a signal was flashed to a military unit at the Dudley Observatory on Arbor Hill, and a twenty-one-gun salute then welcomed the President to the city."

When Lincoln finally emerged (his military escort was late), "Mayor George Hornell Thacher rode with the newly bearded, stovepipe-hatted President in the horse-drawn barouche, down Broadway and up State Street. WELCOME TO THE CAPITAL OF THE EMPIRE STATE—NO MORE COMPROMISE, a banner proclaimed." Despite this fine welcome, however, Albany went against Lincoln in the 1864 elections.

George Thacher was out of office in 1865 when the train bearing President Lincoln's coffin stopped in Albany for a funeral procession that drew thousands. Thacher would hold the office again—for three more terms. George Thacher was always remembered as a tough politician who could come back strongly after defeat. He was referred to as "that old war-horse of the democracy, who, in years gone by, so often led the party to victory."

The Thachers' political influence in the New York capital

In 1932, at a time when Ebby's drinking was embarrassing the family, John Boyd Thacher II nearly won the Democratic Party's nomination for governor.

---

city is apparent. Just west of Albany, for example, is one of the state's most beautiful parks, named for Ebby's uncle, John Boyd Thacher. It was first established on land donated in 1914 by John's widow. Three members of Ebby's family were mayors of Albany, including Ebby's older brother John Boyd "Jack" Thacher II. Ebby's parents were also highly respected; his father was an important manufacturer, and his mother was a leader in Albany society.

Ebby had four older brothers, in addition to two other Thacher children who had died in childhood. The next oldest, John Boyd Thacher II, was named for his illustrious uncle. He would prove to be a political and business superstar in the same mold. Ebby's other three brothers were George, born 1881, Thomas, born 1884, and Kenelm (Ken), born 1892. George went to Massachusetts and operated a company manufacturing stokers, while Thomas became a stockbroker in New York and Detroit. Ken, like his brother Jack, continued to reside in the Albany area and would also serve as Ebby's occasional benefactor in later years.

Not surprisingly, Jack Thacher was the family's outstanding student at Albany Academy, a private school (which is locally referred to as AA!), though George and Thomas also did well. Jack was secretary of the Beck Literary Society and played baseball, football, and hockey. In the military training unit at Albany Academy, he was captain of a company in the battalion.

It is through Ken and his son Ken, Jr., that the Thacher line continues in the Albany area today. Ken's grandson, John Boyd Thacher III, is currently living in nearby Troy and completing his law studies.

Ebby, like Jack, also belonged to the Beck Literary Society, but he did not participate in sports. He took an interest in the military program, however, and was both a corporal and a sergeant. While he never served in U.S. military forces, as Bill Wilson did, there's some evidence that Ebby had the necessary physical stamina and aptitudes to become a good soldier.

Albany Academy is still flourishing in the city. Founded in 1813, the Academy is described as an independent college-preparatory day school, a mission it carries out so well today that all of its 1996 graduates enrolled in a college or university. Three of Ebby's brothers attended Princeton, and Jack went on to earn a law degree at Albany Law School.

The Academy record shows that Ebby entered the E Class in 1903 and exited the school without graduation in June 1915.

While Ebby's performance in school may have been lacking, his talks before AA groups many years later suggested that in his view the Academy may have treated him unfairly. He spent one of his high school years at Burr and Burton in Manchester, Vermont, but was not given credit for this work when he returned to Albany Academy. His resentment over this may have been a factor in his decision to quit school without completing enough courses to graduate.

Ebby was born in Albany, New York, on April 29, 1896. He came into the world with the proverbial silver spoon. Even his given name, Edwin Throckmorton Thacher, had an upper-class sound. There's no family knowledge today of how he

---

The rumor still persists that when Ebby was observed in the middle of a drinking bout, he was mistakenly believed to be Jack—an error of identification that could not have greatly pleased the older brother!

---

came to be called "Ebby," which was sometimes spelled "Ebbie" by friends corresponding with or about him. It's possible, however, that "Ebby" might have been adopted because the family considered it more genteel than the customary "Eddie."

He was the youngest in the family and was said to resemble Jack.

Ebby was undoubtedly both the baby and the pet of the family as he grew up in Albany during the early 1900s. His four older brothers were energetic and active boys who must have awed him with their skills and antics. Ebby's father and three of his brothers became heavy drinkers, but none would hit the depths that Ebby did in later years. During Ebby's early years, the family lived at 111 Washington Avenue, an "elite" street where wealthy merchants and professionals built their homes in the nineteenth century.

Ebby would have been looked upon as a privileged youngster while he was growing up. Bill Wilson was also more privileged than other boys his age in East Dorset. But Ebby's environment was New York State's capital city, where he would have enjoyed prestige stemming from his family's high position in business and politics. Bill's hometown was a village of about three hundred that was rural in its outlook. While Bill's grandfather was the most affluent man in East Dorset and treated Bill well, he had neither the sophistication nor the standing of the Thachers.

Fayette Griffith took considerable pride in having been a Union soldier at the Battle of Gettysburg, and in 1913 Bill accompanied him back to that area for a fiftieth anniversary commemoration of that famous Civil War battle.

Ebby: The Man Who Sponsored Bill W.

Despite their privileges, Ebby and Bill both lived under family pressures. In Ebby's case, he grew up in the shadow of an older brother who set an example in school that Ebby could not hope to match. In Bill's case, he lived with a grandfather who doted on him but also helped foster the idea that Bill had to be number one in everything he did. Both Ebby and Bill would find temporary answers along the way in alcohol, a seeming friend who would also betray them.

3

Summer People in Manchester

Bill Wilson and Ebby Thacher met around 1911 in Manchester, Vermont, where Bill had become known as a leading pitcher on a local baseball team. Bill recalled that he held the wealthy summer people in awe. There's little doubt that he was impressed by Ebby and his brothers and liked being part of their circle. Lois Wilson, who became Bill's wife in 1918, was also from summer people, the Burnhams. She remembered that Ebby was actually closer to her brother Rogers, and Bill was closer to Ebby's brother Ken while they were growing up.

Bill explained in 1954 how summer people differed from those native to his home village, East Dorset. "Lois was the daughter of a very dominating father and she was 4½ years older than I," he said. "Moreover, she represented areas in which I had always felt a great inferiority. Her people were of a fine family in Brooklyn. They were what we Vermonters called city folks. She had social graces of which I knew nothing. People still ate with their knives around me, the back door step was still a lavatory. So, her encouragement of me and her interest in me did a tremendous amount to buck me up."

Ebby had early memories of Manchester, where his family rented a summer cottage just across from Lois's family. At first the Thachers traveled from Albany to Manchester by train, an easy trip. Later on they made it by automobile, a tough trip at first. He remembered his father and brothers arriving in a car they had partly constructed in their rail parts factory; it broke down so often that the sixty-mile trip took several days. (This was the early 1900s; no car worked reliably for any length of time.)

Then, as now, Manchester was a lovely resort town lying in the Battenkill Valley between the Green Mountains to the east and the Taconic Range to the west. Like most of southern Vermont, Manchester's roots go back to colonial times. Edwin L. Bigelow and Nancy H. Otis, local writers and historians, noted that Manchester was chartered in 1761. It already had nearly 1,300 inhabitants thirty years later. It started to attract tourists in the 1850s and quickly became a celebrated summer resort.

Manchester is still a place for summer people.

This summer population, Otis explains, became the lifeblood of the community. "Deeper rooted, richer and steadier, Manchester's 'summer people' have become completely identified with the town," she wrote. "In fact, some of the families have been coming to Manchester for so long that it takes a real old-timer to tell just who is a native."

The Thachers were certainly in this group of Manchester's summer residents who seemed almost like natives. They

---

Manchester's famous visitors include the widows of Abraham Lincoln and Ulysses S. Grant. Robert Todd Lincoln, the only son of Abraham Lincoln to reach adulthood, owned a 412-acre summer estate there called "Hildene." Its huge mansion has been authentically restored and is kept open for visitors. Manchester is also the home of the Orvis Company, known for its high-quality fly fishing equipment. (Bill would also be in awe of the Orvis family.)

---

were coming to Manchester when Ebby was a small child. After renting for years, Ebby's father finally bought a home there in 1923. George Thacher was a leader in Manchester. In 1899 he was a signer of the proposal for incorporation of the Ekwanok Country Club, which is still highly regarded in golfing circles.

The fairways at Ekwanok also would have seen the famous "Lincoln Foursome." The foursome was composed of Robert Todd Lincoln, Robert M. Janney of Philadelphia, and Horace G. Young and George H. Thacher of Albany. Lois's father, Dr. Clark Burnham, was also prominent in Manchester and frequently played golf with men from this foursome.

The Burnhams and the Thachers were close friends during Ebby's childhood. Lois recalled that her family spent nearly half the year in their Manchester summer home. Her father was a prominent Brooklyn physician. But since many of his patients followed him to Manchester, he could afford to take a long vacation there. And it was in Manchester where Lois and Bill met and were betrothed.

Ebby and Bill became better acquainted during the year Ebby lived in Manchester and attended Burr and Burton, a semiprivate school that also serves as Manchester's high school. Ebby boarded with a Congregational minister's family

---

To play at Ekwanok Country Club is a sign that one has arrived. Bill Wilson, in his personal story in the AA Big Book, told of contracting "golf fever" in 1929 and going at once to the country "to carom around the exclusive course which had inspired such awe in me as a lad. I acquired the impeccable coat of tan one sees upon the well-to-do. The local banker watched me whirl fat checks in and out of his till with amused skepticism."

---

that winter—a hint that his parents believed he needed another influence in his life.

But as Ebby told an audience at the Second International Convention in St. Louis in 1955, living with the minister's family was a positive experience. His friendship with the Reverend Sidney Perkins's family and their son Roger was one of the high points of his early years. Roger gave him "many fine ideas about life," Ebby said. "He was a splendid chap. We spent a good many hours talking together." And even in 1955, there was a sad note in Ebby's voice as he explained that Roger joined naval aviation during World War I and was killed while flying at Pensacola, Florida.

Despite Perkins's influence, there is an impression that Ebby was viewed in Manchester as a somewhat mischievous and spoiled child. One elderly Manchester woman who remembered him said, "Yes, I knew the little monkey." Lois, interviewed in 1980, recalled an incident when Ebby and her brother Rogers got lost. "When we lived in Manchester, I remember

The Thacher home on Taconic Avenue
in Manchester, Vermont.

that one day Mrs. Thacher came over to see my mother and said that Ebby hadn't come home. It was getting on towards suppertime and he hadn't come home and she was wondering if he was over at our house. And my brother, Rogers, wasn't home either, and they began to wonder and look around to see."

Lois couldn't remember how old Ebby and Rogers were.

But, Ebby, as you know, had older brothers; the older brothers had gone out on a camping trip up the top of the mountain, the top of the Green Mountain, and apparently, Ebby and Rogers, my brother, had not been allowed to go with them, and their noses were broken [they were resentful]. They wanted to go.

So, after the brothers had started off, apparently—we found this out later, many hours of searching later, both mothers being really concerned about where the boys could be—it occurred to somebody, and I have a feeling it was me, I had heard that the boys were going up camping up to the top of the mountain, that it just might be that the younger kids might have followed them.

So, at night, it had gotten to be dark, my dad and Pa Thacher started up the mountain looking for the boys. And, they went all the way up to the top of the mountain to where the camp was, and there they found them sound asleep. The older brothers wanted them to go back but it was dark by then, and they didn't know what to do so they let them sleep there.

While Ebby may have been troublesome at times, his Manchester summers were a wonderful time in his life. His family was well off and able to afford most of the things they needed. There was swimming, hiking, and fishing. One photo of a youthful Ebby shows him with a large fish, though it didn't appear to be a kind that would be caught either in the Battenkill

River or nearby Lake Emerald. Somebody observed that Ebby was always something of a jokester and might have brought the fish from another locality simply for the photograph!

As Ebby grew older, he also joined in the social life around Manchester. He was readily accepted as a member of a prominent family. He pursued romantic attachments, but according to Lois, he was turned down by a young woman he wanted to marry. Years later, Lois believed, he was still blaming this woman and the rejection for his subsequent troubles!

Though Ebby was from Albany, Manchester played an important role in his future and the events that shaped pre-AA history. It was here that he had met Bill and would meet the men who brought him into the Oxford Group and sobriety. Just south of Manchester was the historic town of Bennington and, further south, Williamstown, Massachusetts, which would

Ebby as a young adult in Manchester. The fish, perhaps caught far from the area, may have been obtained as a prank.

be a center of Oxford Group activity in the mid-1930s. This activity would reach up into the Bennington-Arlington area in Vermont and find Ebby at a low point in his life.

But he had lots of drinking and foolish escapades ahead of him before reaching that critical point in his life. And much of this would be in Albany.

4

Golden Days in Albany

Ebby took what he considered to be his first drink, in Albany in 1914, at age nineteen. He was able to walk into the Hotel Ten Eyck and order a glass of beer at the bar. He remembered having wine at home, but it was this first drink he ordered on his own that seemed significant. It was a wonderful experience, he thought, and his drinking grew from then on.

The Ten Eyck, with a name reflecting Albany's Dutch origins, was then one of Albany's finest hotels. To Ebby, it must have seemed a sign of achieving manhood to be able to drink there. But there would be times when Ebby would no longer be welcome at the Ten Eyck or other Albany drinking places.

Some of his earliest drinking experiences were often with other boys in school, he said many years later. It would be "limited to going downtown and having three or four drinks and getting back at a reasonable hour, eleven o'clock or so, so our families wouldn't suspect anything."

One of Ebby's early drinking companions was a school friend who helped Ebby launch his drinking career. He would phone Ebby up and say, "Eb, let's go get a chocolate milk." Ebby would then repeat this so his family could hear it, thus starting what he later admitted was "the first deceit." They would meet down on the corner and hustle downtown to visit two or three of their haunts, have a few drinks, and go home, Ebby said.

31

"The next spring, I won a cup in a Manual of Arms competition," he said, noting that Albany Academy was a military school, "and boy-like, we went downtown to Keeler's Restaurant and I had to fill that cup with beer many, many times."

Keeler's was a famous restaurant, and it's hard to believe that underage boys could have freely ordered beer there. But it may have been the very prominence of their families that enabled Ebby and his friends to celebrate in this manner.

But it didn't work out well for Ebby.

> The upshot of that was that I got in wrong with the school authorities who heard about the binge and while I wasn't expelled, the principal, who was a lovable old man, wrote my father that he thought the school couldn't do any more for me.

So Ebby dropped out of Albany Academy without graduating. He would never return to school, and yet he often impressed his friends as being well educated. Even Lois Wilson said this, though she tended to be critical of Ebby in other ways. He undoubtedly improved his mind and his vocabulary through occasional reading and association with other members of his family. He also received a good basic education during his years at Albany Academy, even if he never graduated.

Since Ebby was no longer in school and was apparently drifting, his father made one decision for him.

> That fall, the fall of 1915, my father said, "You'd better go work in the foundry." Which I did—I was nineteen then. Well, of course . . . I had started drinking and mostly limited it to Saturday nights, because working in a molding shop, I couldn't do much drinking at night and still get up at seven o'clock. But the drinking would get out of hand every once in a while and I might be a little late for work.

As a son of the owner, Ebby could probably get away with being late for work at times. But he did remember that one of the firm's employees warned him about it.

> I remember we had a man, a grand old man, who was made night watchman for a time, but because of drinking himself, he had injured his leg and we had to put him on the day watch, where he watched the time clock as the men came in in the morning. I remember the first morning I was late, he gave me hell for being late. He said, "Don't start that. It's awful easy to get in the habit."

It's interesting that Ebby recalled this warning nearly forty years later, perhaps with the thought that he should have listened to such people more often. He continued to work for the family firm, however, and eventually moved into a management position. He also continued to drink, and not always with the best results.

> Well, things went on, and my drinking began to get worse. It was mostly social in the beginning. We had a lot of fun, I've got to admit that. And the boys and girls would get together, although there was very little drinking in those days where there were any girls. It simply wasn't done. It wasn't until after World War I that the bars were let down, and drinking was common, as everybody knows, during Prohibition. After Prohibition started, I would drink with the men, my male friends, but also at dances and various parties and sometimes I could drink and take a whole lot of older men home and stow them with their wives, but other times it would get the best of me quickly. I was an in-and-outer from the beginning. Sometimes I could handle it, and sometimes I couldn't.

In the meantime, the Thachers took important leadership roles in the city. Albany proclaimed itself to be America's oldest city when it celebrated its tercentenary in 1924, setting 1624 as the date of its founding by Dutch settlers. Jack Thacher, already an important city official by 1924, wrote the foreword for the official narrative of the Albany tercentenary, while his father, George H. Thacher, composed a sonnet to "The First Americans" for the same publication. George's poem eulogized the early American Indians as persons who did not know how to lie or steal and being of innate virtue. It ended with the thought that "in these Red Men no evil could reside."

The 1920s were a prosperous period for the country, but it was also a time of turmoil over the drinking issue. Ebby and Bill, like most of the pioneering AA members, would actually do much of their drinking during national Prohibition, which lasted from January 1920 until December 1933. (Bill, in all of his drinking, had only about three years of legal imbibing.) In the meantime, both Albany and New York City had plenty of speakeasy establishments and other bootleggers, so getting liquor was hardly ever a problem. As William Kennedy noted in *O Albany!*:

> Prohibition in Albany was a contradiction in terms. Very little was ever prohibited in this city, which has always had a mind to do what it wanted to do and never mind the civil law, or the moral law, either. Albany was always a place where you could restore your spirit or smudge your soul.

But if getting liquor wasn't a problem, Ebby's drinking was, and he noted how it progressed:

> As time went on, it began to get worse, and I did a lot of drinking in Manchester, Vermont, too. Of course, I saw Bill off and on during these years, after his return from service abroad during World War I. I saw him in Manchester occasionally, and I must admit, the times that I saw him, I was

doing most of the drinking and he hadn't started in yet. It wasn't until later on that Bill really started to drink heavily. I would come to New York once in a while, and as he has mentioned in his talks, most of the time when I hit New York, I was drunk.

The time frame here is somewhat difficult to establish. Bill took his first drink during World War I while serving as an army lieutenant at Fort Rodman in New Bedford, Massachusetts. He drank frequently in the early 1920s. He even said that while taking a law course, he was too drunk to think or write at one of the final exams. He was certainly a serious problem drinker by 1926 or 1927, though this might not have been obvious to most people. Since Ebby would often telephone the Wilsons while drunk, this may have created the impression that his problem was more serious than Bill's. In fact, however, both of them progressed rapidly into alcoholism in the 1920s.

In the meantime, Ebby had lost his job when the Thacher company closed in 1922. He had been listed as purchasing agent of the company, while his brother Thomas was vice-president and general manager and Ken was production manager. In his taped memories, Ebby mentioned working for the firm but was less specific about his duties there.

If he did serve as a real purchasing agent, Ebby's later employment record gave little evidence of developing professional skills that would have won him a position with another firm. At one time during World War II, he would serve as an assistant purchasing agent, but it didn't last long. Bill would say, in fact, that one of Ebby's problems was that the family money didn't run out until Ebby was about forty. By that time it was almost too late to learn an occupation.

Why did the Thacher firm close after seventy years of operation? Ebby later said that the foundry folded up due to "changing conditions" and that his father was a man who "was set in his ways" and didn't want to adjust himself to the business demands of the competition. Ebby's nephew, Ken Thacher, Jr., believed the failure was due to excessive losses resulting from some ill-advised government contracts during World War I. Ken added, however, that George Thacher still had considerable assets following the company's failure and was able to leave each of his sons about $150 thousand upon his death in 1929.

In 1929 dollars, $150 thousand was a fortune, but all of the brothers eventually had financial problems. Ken Thacher, Jr., said that the brothers lost some of their money in the 1929 crash. It's also likely that Ebby squandered some of his inheritance during drunken escapades. Three of the other brothers developed drinking problems, but none had troubles to the extent Ebby did. Perhaps his descent into alcoholism and destitution even made them feel they didn't really have problems!

After the closing of the Thacher company, Ebby tried selling insurance and then went to work in an Albany brokerage office. But by his own account, he did little work, and he left no record of his actual performance or earnings.

In Ebby's view, his drinking hadn't been too serious in the 1920s. He recalled:

> At that time, my drinking was not so bad. When I was home with the family, I had the responsibility, of course, and I limited my drinking to, oh, once every two or three months, I would go off maybe on a party for the boys. And that's about all it was.

His joining the brokerage office, however, seemed to be a turning point. It was the Albany office of John Nickerson, a New York investment house. "All the bond salesmen, security salesmen, would meet every afternoon at one or two places and start drinking," Ebby said. "Also, we'd make out our reports where we said that we reported progress—which meant progress alcoholically, when you come right down to it! Perhaps we made one or two calls in the morning, and that was it."

Ebby, by his own admission, was apparently coasting along in a position without really being productive, despite the high volume of trading in stocks and bonds in those boom years immediately preceding the Great Crash. This can mean only that his earnings were very low if he worked on commission or that the office was poorly managed if it permitted such lackluster performance on the part of its salesmen. Either way, Ebby's outlook for a long-term future in stock and bond trading was likely to be very limited.

The city directories of Albany for the 1920s show several addresses for Ebby. In the 1924–25 period, he resided at 830 Myrtle Avenue, which was also the residence of Jack and Lulu Thacher, as well as Ken and Thomas. During 1927 and 1928 he was shown as a salesman residing at 5 Elk Street, with a business address of 100 State Street. His residence was listed as 248 State Street in the 1929–30 period, with no business address listed. Then, in 1930–31 he was shown as back at Jack's residence on Myrtle Avenue.

In the meantime, Ebby lost two important anchors in his life with the passing of his parents in the late 1920s.

My mother died in the spring of 1927, and she was followed two years later by my father. Along about this time, I think it was shortly after my father's death, [while] I was still with John Nickerson . . . that Bill arrived in Albany en route to Vermont. He called me up—this was on a Saturday—and Bill suggested that I meet him downtown and we'd take on a couple of drinks, never having had a drink together, which we did.

Here was a curious fact: Despite their early friendship and occasional contacts, Bill and Ebby had not drunk together. Bill seems to have believed that they did and even mentioned it in his personal accounts, but Ebby was always quite clear on that point. It may be that Bill had confused certain social occasions, such as those in Manchester, with "drinking together." Bill may also have remembered drinking with Ebby's brother Ken, and in time remembered it as drinking with Ebby. But on this matter, we can probably believe Ebby: They really shared only one drinking bout.

But the drinking bout they shared was so spectacular that it may have seemed to be a number of drunks wrapped into one. In today's terms, it would be like starting in a hotel bar and ending up with a ride on the space shuttle!

One reason for the way it worked out is that early aviation had been established in Albany, and Ebby had been attracted to it. An Albany history noted that famed aviator Charles Lindbergh was cheered by thousands of Albanians in 1927 when he made an appearance there in Lincoln Park. A year later, when Albany created the first city-owned airport in the nation, it was named "Lindbergh Field" and was located at the site of the present Albany County Airport.

As the younger brother of Albany's mayor (Jack had just taken office), it's likely that thirty-one-year-old Ebby Thacher was one of the thousands who greeted the Lone Eagle on his Albany visit. Lindbergh's sensational trip across the Atlantic may also have sparked Ebby's interest in aviation, as it did for so many other young Americans.

Ebby started to hang out with pilots at the airport, and some of them became drinking cronies. And he finally enlisted his old Manchester friend Bill Wilson in a sixty-mile flight that could have been as dangerous as Lindbergh's feat, if only because Ebby, Bill, and perhaps the pilot were apparently inebriated while crossing rough terrain with threatening air currents.

Thus, when Bill called that Saturday in January 1929, Ebby was already an aviation enthusiast as well as a drinking buddy of several pilots.

> And at that time, I was playing around in Albany with a bunch of flyers who were barnstormers at the Albany airport. They called themselves Flyers Incorporated. Bill and I attended a party at the house of one of the pilots.
>
> As I said, Bill was headed for Vermont the next day, and I couldn't see why Bill would have to take that two-by-four railroad up there. Why not hire a plane? So I made a deal with a boy, one Ted Burke, to fly us up the next day. I put Bill in the hotel that night, and I went out and drank all night, so I would be sure to make the trip. I went around and picked him up the next morning, got Ted Burke out of bed and out to the airport, and we flew him to Manchester and landed on an airstrip about the size of a postage stamp. I often think that Ted was awfully good-natured to fly two drunks up there. Of course, word had gotten around that we were on our way up, and half the town of Manchester was out there. Bill and I ducked for the hangar but fast, and ran into an old friend, who drove us on up to East Dorset, where Bill was going to spend some time with a friend of his. I returned on the evening train to Albany, and right back into the drinking again.

Bill, also in 1954 recollections, had a version of the flight that he reviewed when commenting on Ebby's call on him in 1934.

> In early '29, I remember stopping to see Ebby and he had made the acquaintance of some flying folks. We had had an all-night party and then chartered a plane and pilot to fly from Albany to Manchester, Vermont. They were working

on a landing field up there, but no planes had appeared, and we called Manchester to tell the folks that we would be the first arrivals. Tight as he was, the pilot was pretty reluctant, but finally off we went. I vaguely remember spotting the town of Bennington through the haze. The excited citizens of Manchester had got together a welcoming committee. The town band had turned out. The town delegation was headed by Mrs. Anna Simonds Orvis (a member of the family that also owned the famous Orvis fly fishing equipment firm), a rather stately and dignified lady, who at that time owned the famous Equinox House.

Bill continued:

> We circled the field. But meantime, all three of us had been pulling at a bottle of liquor, cached in the rear cockpit to the front. Somehow, we lit on the pretty bumpy meadow. The delegation charged forward. It was up to Ebby and me to do something, but we could do absolutely nothing. We somehow slid out of the cockpit, fell on the ground, and there we lay, immobile. Such was the history-making episode of the first airplane ever to light at Manchester, Vermont.

Bill had come to Manchester to visit his old friend Mark Whalon, a rural mail carrier who lived in East Dorset and had been almost like an uncle to him during his teenage years.

> After a time I found myself at the home of my old friend the postman. The next day, a frightful hangover, a crying jag, in which I wandered all over East Dorset. Then a letter of abject apology to Mrs. Orvis.

Though Bill's version of the trip was similar to Ebby's, there are significant differences. Ebby didn't mention that the pilot might have been drunk too, and he didn't seem to have experienced the kind of remorse that beset Bill the following day. But whether the pilot was drinking or just recovering from an all-night party, even this short flight over rough terrain to a just-completed airport was risky and ill advised.

On the other hand, it was the sort of crazy experience that nobody is likely to forget. It may have been that single flight that gave Bill and Ebby a bonding they'd never had even during their years together in Manchester. If either needed proof that the other was a serious and fully committed drinker, this flight from Albany to Manchester provided it. This was the way 1929 started for them, and before the year was out, both Ebby and Bill would be facing serious troubles with a plunge in the stock market and the beginnings of the Great American Depression. And for both Bill and Ebby, the worst of times was on the way.

5

An Exile in Manchester

New York's 1932 gubernatorial election may have helped place Ebby Thacher back in Manchester, Vermont, where he would eventually meet the three rescuers who would bring him into the Oxford Group.

Ebby explained it this way:

> Several times in Albany, I had been reprimanded by the local authorities that I was drinking too much. My brother [Jack] was a prominent man in town, and I wasn't doing him any good. So in the fall of 1932, I took off for Manchester and lived in the Battenkill Inn for about two years. And of course, the drinking went on up there just the same.

Ebby's admission that he wasn't doing his brother any good was probably an understatement. Jack Thacher had been Albany's mayor since 1926, when he had succeeded William S. Hackett upon his accidental death.

By 1932, Jack had become one of the Democratic party's rising stars, at the very time when the party's chances were suddenly strong. The Republican Hoover Administration in Washington had become fatally linked to the Great Depression and was about to go down in defeat, carrying other Republican officeholders or contenders with it. Franklin D. Roosevelt, the popular governor of New York State, was about to sweep into the White House, bringing one of the great political upheavals of all time. And one of the men favored to replace him as New York's governor was Jack Thacher, an outstanding speaker who was highly visible as the mayor of the state's capital city.

Jack had all the right credentials. His uncle and namesake, the first John Boyd Thacher, had been one of New York State's most prominent leaders and even had a special room named for him in the Library of Congress. Jack himself had placed Al Smith's name in nomination for governor in 1926 and had campaigned for Smith in the 1928 presidential campaign. Indeed, one of the photos published upon Jack's death in 1957 showed him conferring with Franklin D. Roosevelt in 1930, when Roosevelt was still New York's governor. So Jack was the logical person to be in line for the governorship when FDR made his historic bid for the White House.

But the selection of the candidate was up to the nominating convention. After an all-day, behind-the-scenes struggle, the nomination went to Roosevelt's lieutenant governor, Herbert H. Lehman, largely because he had FDR's endorsement and because party leaders wanted a strong connection with the U.S. presidency. (Lehman, a member of a prominent banking family, was governor for ten years and then served in the U.S. Senate.) It was called a near-miss for Jack and also the high-water mark of his political career. Though he served as mayor for another eight years and eventually became a judge, he never came that close again to a higher office.

Jack would hold the office of Albany's mayor until 1940, when he resigned. He would be followed by Erastus Corning II, a leader whose long service in office became an Albany legend.

It would be unfair to say that he lost out because his youngest brother was becoming the town drunk. But it is likely that some of Ebby's problems became identified with the Thacher name. For whatever reasons, Ebby probably had the family's encouragement and assistance when he left Albany that fall to settle in Manchester, a place that was like a second hometown.

During some of this time, Ebby must have had money, either from his inheritance or from the family. He was able to live without working much of the time, and also to afford liquor, though he did stay sober for long intervals.

He also engaged in healthy outdoor activities, as he explained in his 1954 recollections:

> But one winter, the first winter, I think it was, the man who owned the inn had a son who had gotten permission from one of the lumber companies to use a cabin on one of the lumber jobs on top of a mountain range. This man thought it would be a good deal if I went up there and tried to get sobered up and stay sober and do a lot of work around the place, go out and cut trails, and so forth, [to] help the Green Mountain Trail along [a trail that ran three hundred miles north and south, the length of the Green Mountains]. So we went up there. This was, I think, shortly before Christmas. And we stayed up there in this cabin. We did some rabbit hunting with the hounds, went out and cut trails and Saturdays and Sundays, some of the boys would come up weekends with us—no liquor up there, although on the way up, I had two pints of gin which I consumed the first night and that was all we had.

Ebby, during his sober periods, often did physical labor, and he seemed to have enjoyed it most of the time. Spending the winter of 1932–33 in the Green Mountains was the sort of experience he was likely to enjoy. And contributing to the improvement of the Green Mountain Trail must have given him a sense of accomplishment.

Bill and Lois, following Bill's return from army service in World War I, took hiking trips along the trail. Lois said that most of the trail was steep and rugged. She remembered the primitive log cabins that were five or ten miles apart, which hikers could use. There was also a cooperative spirit among users of the trail. She wrote:

> The law of the camp required occupants to leave enough cut wood for the next traveler and to replace with something similar any food found or eaten in the cabin. If drinking water was not at hand, there were instructions to tell where it was located.

The purpose in Ebby's going to the mountain cabin was to get away from the drinking, and for a time it worked.

> I stayed up there about six months altogether, and returning to Manchester [Depot], I stayed sober for two or three months more, when I again fell off the wagon. [Manchester is separate from the Manchester Depot—a distance of two miles.] In the meantime, I had lost my friend, the owner of the inn, who was suddenly stricken with a heart attack. I went on all that summer, drinking off and on, the winter also, and the following spring, I moved up to the town of Manchester itself. I stayed at a tourist place a friend of mine ran and I opened up the family home. One of my brothers wanted to live up there. Most of the furniture had been taken out but there was enough there to equip one room, the room I had occupied formerly, and I stayed there, doing a lot of drinking, of course, living alone and moody and brooding, thinking of things all the time.

These recollections covered the period between early 1933 and mid-1934—a time when Ebby's frequent drinking bouts were marking him as a troublemaker in Manchester.

One story that has grown up over the years is that Ebby, about 1934, got drunk and drove his father's car into a house where an older couple was living. He then stepped out, so the story goes, and asked the couple for a cup of coffee with just a little cream and only one sugar. There was such an incident, according to one of Ebby's friends, but it happened much earlier. And it may have been Jack's car that Ebby was driving, since Ebby's father had died in 1929. In any case, Ebby no longer had access to any family member's car by 1934.

Such incidents, in a small town, were quickly making Ebby a pariah. Coupled with two arrests for drunkenness, this would lead to serious trouble late that summer. "I had already gotten in a brush with the law a couple of times, fined five dollars on each occasion. I was told if I was arrested a third time for intoxication, it might go hard on me," Ebby recalled in 1954.

The climactic trouble actually started with a painting project for the family home. The house needed painting. Perhaps Jack had even suggested that Ebby could do it while he was living there. Or it might have been Ebby's idea. In any case, broke and alone, Ebby took on a project that was too much for him:

Mary Bort, who was a young child during Ebby's 1933 drinking period, remembers a drunken Ebby coming out to their farm to talk with her father about going fishing. Her aunt quickly shooed her into the house, presumably so she wouldn't hear what Ebby was saying. Her father then took Ebby home.

> I decided I would paint the house, and wrote my brother to that effect, and we had a good sized ladder there, but I was so shaky from drinking I couldn't do it. It was all right on the first three or four rungs of the ladder, but from then on up, I couldn't do a thing.

The Thacher home, still an attractive residence on Manchester's Taconic Avenue, was also quite high, and painting it would have been a challenge even for a professional crew. But he eventually called a professional and was able to finish the project.

But he was about to receive help of another kind—help for his drinking problem. Ebby was about to become reacquainted with a couple of old friends and would make a new one in a movement then called the Oxford Group. His life was about to change in astonishing ways that he couldn't have predicted or planned. And for a while, he would have the best of times.

Cebra, Shep, and Rowland

One idea heard often in AA is that there are no coincidences. This is but another way of saying that even the most astonishing events, though seemingly the result of pure chance, come about through the guidance and direction of God.

Whether divinely ordained or simply the result of luck, the actions that brought Ebby Thacher into the Vermont Oxford Group in 1934 were key steps in the eventual formation of Alcoholics Anonymous. It's possible to say that any number of channels could have been used to bring AA into existence, but one wonders what these could have been. In retrospect, everything that brought the Oxford Group message to Ebby and then to Bill Wilson seems to have meshed perfectly—though this wouldn't have been clear at the time.

Three members of the Oxford Group were instrumental in bringing Ebby into the Oxford Group: Cebra G., Shep C., and Rowland H. Rowland and Shep were personal friends, while Cebra was at least associated with them in the Oxford Group. Cebra also just happened to be the son of a prominent judge in Bennington, Vermont.

While Cebra, Shep, and Rowland all had a role in bringing Ebby into the Oxford Group, it was Rowland who gave Ebby more personal assistance and actually provided what AA members would call sponsorship. Years later, Ebby would mention his gratitude for these men's work and would point out that they were also important to the founding of AA because they had given him the message that he would convey to Bill.

Rowland has been a "mystery man" in AA history because he apparently never took part in the early AA work or had an interest in the fellowship. Like Ebby, however, he was an important link in the chain of individuals who contributed to AA's origins. Rowland appears in the chapter titled "There Is a Solution" in *Alcoholics Anonymous* as the American businessman who went to Europe in 1931 to seek treatment from the eminent psychiatrist Carl Jung.

Rowland was a Yale graduate and a member of an old Rhode Island family with colonial roots going back to 1635 (the year the first Thachers also arrived in America). He appeared to be a likely candidate for recovery. But when the treatment failed to help Rowland maintain continuous sobriety, Jung suggested that his only hope for recovery might be in seeking and finding a vital spiritual experience of some kind.

This was in itself a remarkable suggestion that could have come only from the Jungian view, since the more popular Freudian and Adlerian schools had little room for religious conversion experiences.

Rowland followed up on Jung's suggestion by joining the Oxford Group, either in Europe or upon his return to the

---

One early AA member in Detroit used to say in his talks that Rowland really tried to see Sigmund Freud before getting in touch with Jung, though there's no evidence to support this belief. But if Rowland had consulted Freud, it's not likely that the great Austrian psychoanalyst would have told him to seek help in religion, as Jung suggested.

United States. He found his answer and, as the Big Book stated when it was first published in 1939, "he lives and is a free man."

Ebby, in recollections taped nearly twenty years later, had this to say about his 1934 contacts with the three men and the message they carried. The first two to call on him were Cebra and Shep, men he had known for years:

> Well, these fellows told me they had run into a group called the Oxford Group and had gotten some pretty sensible things out of it based on the life of Christ, biblical times. It was really more of a spiritual than it was a religious movement. I listened to what they had to say, and I was very much impressed because it was what I had been taught as a child and what I inwardly believed, but had lain aside.

This reference to childhood teachings is a strong indication that Ebby had been impressed and influenced by his family's church attendance while he was growing up. The Thacher family had both Episcopalian and Presbyterian connections, and Ebby's mother was listed as a member of the First Reformed Church upon her death in 1927. Since Ebby had also lived with the Reverend Sidney Perkins family in Manchester during one of his school years, he had undoubtedly received further religious teaching there. This apparently helped make

---

There has been little information about Rowland published by AA World Services; however, the *AA Grapevine* featured an excellent article about him in May 1995, by Ron R. of Bowling Green, Kentucky. Rowland's recovery was also discussed in a 1961 exchange of letters between Bill Wilson and Carl Jung; these can be found on pp. 276–81 of *The Language of the Heart*, available from the AA Grapevine, Inc.

---

him receptive and understanding as he listened to his two visitors.

In a 1961 talk in San Jose, California, Ebby recalled that "they talked a lot of sense with me, they left a book with me. They said, now, you've been trying to run your life your own way, down on your luck, not getting anywhere, drinking yourself to death, why don't you try turning your life over to God?"

Ebby's first two Oxford Group contacts were abstaining from drinking, as the Group implicitly required of its members without directly demanding it. Ebby didn't view their drinking as being similar to his. "They weren't alcoholics in the sense that I am," he recalled in 1961. "They both drank heavily. They were more or less power hungry, both of them. One [Shep C.] was a New York stockbroker, and he just wanted to have the world by the horns so he could run it."

Cebra, an attorney whose family was reportedly wealthy, eventually moved to France to become a permanent resident there until his death in 1979. He would, however, play an indirect role in a 1953 action that would take Ebby to Texas.

It was perhaps remarkable that two such power drivers as Cebra and Shep would even take the time to call on a person who was rapidly becoming Manchester's town drunk, even if he was an old friend. This was the way the Oxford Group members worked, however. It also set the pattern for the way the soon-to-be-born AA fellowship would work.

Shep C. had scored successes in the stock market, although his fortunes may have been temporarily on the wane in 1934. Though he never "ran the world," Shep did become a colonel during World War II and later rose to a high executive position in a major corporation based in Milwaukee.

What prompted these Oxford Group members to think about Ebby Thacher as a prospect for their program? Cebra recorded his memories of this for Bill Wilson in 1954.

Cebra was a young lawyer in Bennington in the early 1930s, and he was not getting along well with his father, the judge. Cebra recalled meeting Rowland H. at a party in his parents' home in 1934. Later on, Cebra had a fight with his father and walked out of the office without even locking the door. Walking south toward Williamstown, Massachusetts, he caught a ride with Rowland, who took him to another Oxford Group member's home. There he was introduced to the Group principles.

> . . .They, as I remember, almost guaranteed that if I'd accept the principles of the Group, that this burden of drink, I believe they called it, would be lifted from me. I did get into the Oxford Group. . . . It was perfectly true I didn't stop drinking because that didn't seem to be required, but I did seem, at least, to drink moderately for quite a while. This [was] around June 1934.

Cebra mentions "moderate" drinking. This suggests that he may have been a rebellious young man who was doing a lot of drinking as a way of not conforming. But perhaps he was not an alcoholic as AA understands the condition.

Cebra went to New York and visited the Oxford Group meetings there. He was so defiant at first that he even went to

---

Stopping drinking wasn't required in the Oxford Group, but it was *implied*. Oxford Groupers also believed that alcoholics would return to drinking if they didn't stop smoking, a belief that wasn't adopted in AA.

---

his first meeting with a quart of whiskey in the large hip pocket of a special tailor-made suit.

> I wasn't really trying to hide it either. I was a little bit rugged about the whole thing. After I became sober, or on my own, a seemingly normal drinker for a while, I came back to Bennington and tried to make amends to my parents and follow the principles of the Oxford Group.

Cebra said that he visited Rowland H. at Rowland's home near Arlington. Shep C. was also there. While they were swimming in the pool, they decided to do some missionary work in the Oxford Group manner.

> I then remembered Ebby Thacher, whom I had known for many years in Manchester. I had gone there to play golf, etc., for a very long time.

He suggested to Shep that they should go over to see Ebby.

Cebra recalled that the other two men were not anxious to go and that, at one point, he had to push a little. Rowland didn't go for some reason, but Shep finally agreed to join him.

> We went to the Thacher house. Ebby was sitting out in the back veranda and there were the usual tin cans the drunkard is always surrounded with, his suit was pretty dirty, and he was sitting with his head in his arms.
>
> I walked up and said, "Ebby, having fun?" He said, "Go to hell." I said, "Well, if you don't want to live like this, we have an idea." So one of the first things we did was . . . we got Ebby's suit cleaned, we took him to a restaurant—I suppose we did that before, got him a meal—and we started to talk to him, both Shep and I, on the principles of the Oxford Group.

Cebra went on to say that Shep took Ebby to New York, but this account does not seem to agree with either Ebby's or Shep's recollections. It's more likely that he was describing here their first meeting with Ebby, and that the trip to New York came weeks later. Later on, following the visit from Cebra and Shep, Rowland H. also got in touch with Ebby.

Ebby was not quite ready to quit drinking when Cebra and Shep called on him, and he was also determined to complete painting the house. Ebby said:

> At that time, I again wrote my brother and made a deal with a local painter, a boss painter, who sent me one of his men, a fellow I liked, and some equipment, so that we could really get up and paint the house. He and I tackled it and we gave it two coats—we did a good job.

This was a trait that Ebby would display again and again, despite his generally poor employment record. He did devote himself enthusiastically to whatever work came his way. While others may have considered him lazy and indifferent, there were times when he could focus his attention and energy in highly constructive ways. He was, after all, a member of a high-achieving family, and he did have some of the positive traits that had helped other Thachers succeed so well in business and politics.

He was also subject to mood swings, however, and his enthusiasm for any project tended to die quickly. Of the house painting venture, he said, "But as soon as that was over, and the equipment moved off, I began to lose interest. I had nothing to do. I went right back to the bottle."

It's not known how long he continued to drink or if the Oxford Group men called on him at intervals; it's more likely they left him alone until another crisis occurred.

That came quickly and included a bizarre episode that must have been the talk of the neighborhood. Ebby described it this way:

> One day, it was raining hard, and I happened to look out and saw four or five pigeons that had lighted on the roof. I didn't like that—a new paint job—so I got the old double-barreled shotgun and walked out. It was very slippery on the grass, it had been raining hard. I sat down and from that position, I started blazing away at the pigeons.

The Thacher home was on a street of similarly upscale residences in Manchester. Most of them would have been occupied during the summer. It's easy to believe that the shotgun blasts would have almost caused a panic up and down the street. But with considerable understatement, Ebby explained how the police came to see him: "The neighbors didn't like it and they complained to somebody, so the next day, [the police] were down looking for me, but I was sound asleep and they couldn't get in."

Ebby, according to the way he described the incident later, seemed to consider the shotgun affair as a private matter that had occurred on his own family's property and should have been of no concern to the community!

The local police officers didn't consider the offense serious enough to break into the house and arrest Ebby, but they obviously had orders to take him into custody as soon as he appeared in public, which he did later in the day.

> I went uptown that afternoon and sat on the steps of the hardware store, wondering just what I would do, broke, of course, when this constable came around. . . . He and I had gone to school the same time as Bill had been there. He says, "Sorry, Ebby, but I've got to take you to Bennington."

The policeman, Constable John Jackson, drove Ebby to Bennington, the county seat about twenty-five miles south of Manchester. Ebby was to appear before Judge Collins G., Cebra's father. Despite the long friendship and Ebby's recent contacts with Cebra, there was no reason at this point to believe that Judge G. would show any leniency. Ebby would always mention his dread of Vermont's "habitual drunk" law, which could fetch a person six months' prison time after three arrests for drunkenness. (Other states had similar laws, which have been either withdrawn or not enforced as views about alcoholism have changed.)

Ebby could have been locked up for the weekend, but Judge G. seemed lenient in that respect. "The judge told me that I was due back in Bennington for trial Monday morning," Ebby recalled, "so I told him I would be there."

But Ebby was already thinking about needing a drink.

One of my highlights of the whole thing was the fact that when I got back to Manchester to the house, I had three or four bottles of ale in a cool cellar. The judge said, "I want you back here Monday morning sober." I told him I would be. Well, when I got back there to Manchester, there were these bottles down in the cellar. I said to myself, "Now you've only got three or four bottles down here, and this is Saturday and you won't be able to get any more—if they've sent the word out here in Manchester not to sell you any more—what harm is it going to do to take a bottle of ale?"

It was Ballantine's ale, one of Ebby's favorite brews.

With this kind of reasoning, Ebby probably couldn't get out of the car fast enough when Constable Jackson returned him to the Thacher house. Hearing this story for the first time, AA members today would be expecting Ebby to say that he drank the ale, found further supplies, and ended up in even more trouble with the law.

It didn't work out that way. Something happened in the cellar that proved to be one of those astonishing turning points—a turning point for Ebby, for Bill Wilson, and for all those who followed in recovery. It could be called "Ebby's Miracle." His recollection is emphasized here because it was the key to the events of the next few months that would lead him to Bill:

> *So down I went, and I reached for a bottle of ale, and I couldn't take it. I had said I would be there sober, and this wouldn't exactly be sobriety. I went upstairs and this voice said, "Oh, don't be silly. Go down and get that ale. My God, you're shaking. Go on down and get it." Well, I couldn't do it. It wasn't playing the game square, the way I looked at it. And when I finally made the decision not to touch it and took it over to a friend of mine, three or four houses away, I felt right then a great release from the whole thing. And that lasted for me for over two years. That was the start of the whole release from the problem for the time being.*

Ebby would always describe that moment as a victory, something like a weight being lifted from his shoulders. "I've often thought about it, for many years, when I started drinking again, why I couldn't recapture that feeling I had then," he would say in 1961. He would even use "pink cloud" to describe the wonderful feeling he had following the victory in the cellar. He would also think of it as a "more mature outlook."

Events unfolded swiftly. On Monday Ebby went back before the judge, and a third member of the Oxford Group entered the picture—Rowland H.—a man Ebby had met only shortly before. With Rowland present in the court, the judge gave Ebby a lecture and then asked Rowland if he would assist Ebby. Ebby recalled in 1954:

Rowland H. came to my rescue and said he'd be responsible for me, and the judge released me in his custody. I returned to the house for three or four days and turned off the water and the lights and shut it up for the winter. Then I went down to a town called Shaftsbury, about fifteen miles below Manchester. I spent a week or so with Rowland H., and then we went on down to New York.

In those same recollections, Ebby recorded his memory of Rowland, who had died in 1945. Though the AA system of "sponsorship" and "carrying the message" had yet to be developed with its emphasis on alcoholism, Rowland was practicing it as an Oxford Grouper, particularly in the areas of helping others and seeking guidance through quiet times. Remembering Rowland as a "good guy," Ebby told how his benefactor had come to see him at the Thachers' Manchester home. "The first day he came to see me, he helped me clean up the place," Ebby remembered. "Things were a mess and he helped me straighten it up and he stuck by me from beginning to end. In fact, one time he and I took a trip down through Texas and New Mexico and spent a couple of weeks on a ranch that he owned."

Rowland did own a ranch near Alamagordo, New Mexico, and an article in the *Providence Sunday Journal,* September 20, 1931, even detailed his success in discovering potters' clay in that part of New Mexico and putting it to commercial use. Since this was also the year of Rowland's first or second visit to Carl Jung, the article conveys the impression that Rowland was either staying sober by this time or at least was managing to carry on his business interests even while drinking.

Cebra G., who recorded his own memories for AA in 1954, said that Rowland had been driving in Massachusetts from South Williamstown to Pittsfield when he heard an inner voice say, "You will never take a drink again." Rowland then threw his pint bottle, a constant companion, into the bushes along the road, according to the account Cebra remembered.

In any case, Rowland was sober and actively carrying the Oxford Group message by the time of his meeting with Ebby. He told Ebby about his sessions with Jung. Ebby recalled:

> He thought that Jung had really gotten under his skin and was going to help him, but something happened to Rowland as soon as he returned to the States—he went right back to drinking. He returned for further treatment with Jung, who told him at the time, as I recall it, that he thought that he was hopeless. So Rowland came back and was rather dejected, downcast until he ran across this Oxford Group. Religion was the only thing that would help to get rid of his drinking problem. Rowland was impressed by the simplicity of the early Christian teachings as advocated by the Oxford Group, and he really lived with them and practiced them himself.
>
> Of course, Carl Jung had impressed [Rowland] with the scientific approach as well as the religious approach to the problem of alcoholism, and I think that Rowland was very much taken with this idea and hooked it up so as to combine . . . physiologically and temperamentally the difficulty

In the summer of 1935, with Ebby sober and living in a mission in New York City, Rowland took him on a two-week trip to the Alamagordo ranch. Ebby would recall at the 1954 Texas State Conference that Rowland had a small Oxford Group meeting on the patio of his ranchhouse, attended by ten or twelve people from neighboring farms and ranches. Ebby didn't think they sobered anybody up or converted anybody, but it was probably the first meeting of its kind in the Southwest.

that a man experienced who was inclined as an alcoholic. Rowland continued the remainder of his life his close connection and association with the Oxford Group. He attended a great many of the so-called house parties in different parts of the country and was always active until the time of his death.

Ebby, in addition to finding sobriety and sponsorship, was also called upon to help pass along the Oxford Group message. Even after going to New York, he returned to Vermont with other members—perhaps Shep and Rowland—and spoke at a junior college, two churches, a town meeting hall, and someplace else, all in two afternoons and two nights. "And I gave out more than I talked about," he would say. "I felt good about the whole thing, and felt that these guys must have something, and that there must be a Higher Power."

On these trips, Rowland set a great example.

During my subsequent traveling around the New England states with him, Rowland gave me a great many things that were of a great value to me later on. He had had a thorough indoctrination and he passed as much of this on to me as he could. When we took trips together we would get up early in the morning, and before we even had any coffee, we would sit down and try to rid ourselves of any thoughts of the material world and see if we couldn't find out the best plan for our lives for that day and to follow whatever guidance came to us.

I am grateful for all that Rowland did for me. He impressed upon me the four principles of the Oxford Group, which were Absolute Honesty, Absolute Purity, Absolute Unselfishness, Absolute Love. He was particularly strong in advocating the Absolute Honesty—honesty with yourself, honesty with your fellow man, honesty with God. These things he followed himself and thereby by example, he made me believe in them again as I had as a young man.

These were the ideas Ebby was picking up in the closing months of 1934. The experience already had made a profound difference in his attitude and behavior. But to his Oxford Group friends, this was not unusual. All around the world in the 1930s, the Oxford Group was enjoying remarkable success in changing people's lives for the better. Founded by a Lutheran minister named Frank Buchman, who had himself undergone a sweeping spiritual transformation in 1908, the Group advocated first-century Christian principles and managed to bridge most of the religious differences of the times. The Oxford Group had a broader mission than helping alcoholics, but its message enabled many problem drinkers to find sobriety.

Now, in helping Ebby Thacher, the Oxford Group had reached the person who would carry the message to Bill Wilson. Ebby had found the Oxford Group program in a place where it was enjoying unusual success in 1934.

In the meantime, colder weather had set in, he had closed the house in Manchester, and Rowland had driven him to New York City, where he stayed for a time with Shep C. in his apartment.

Ebby, probably with Shep's help, found lodging at Calvary Mission in lower Manhattan. He was destitute, but he had the advantage now of sobriety and a new outlook. Even in his destitute state, he would somehow be able to scrape together a few nickels. One nickel would be for a call to Lois Wilson, another would be for a later call to Bill, and the third nickel would be for a subway ride to Brooklyn to call on his old friend from their Manchester days. It would be money well spent—in time it would lead to the recovery of more than two million alcoholics.

7

A Resident at Calvary Mission

While Ebby was recovering in Vermont in the late summer of 1934, Bill Wilson, in Brooklyn, was making a desperate, last-ditch effort to deal with his own problems. His personal story in the AA Big Book describes a process of attempted recovery that's common to many alcoholics. His first hope had been in self-knowledge: understanding his alcoholism and realizing that even one drink would lead to disaster. Then he had walked into a bar "to use the telephone" and found himself getting drunk, seemingly for no reason. He had explored other avenues of recovery and had even been able to discuss his problem with total strangers. But he always drank again, and on Armistice Day, 1934 (now Veterans Day), he started on yet another binge.

Ebby, the man who would be his sponsor, was two hundred miles north in Manchester that summer, and there was no real personal reason why he should have come to New York. After all, his roots were in Albany, only about sixty miles west of Manchester, and now that he was sober there was little reason why his family wouldn't warmly welcome him back. And since he needed employment, his influential older brother Jack Thacher, with important contacts throughout the community, could help him. Jack was, of course, in excellent community standing as Albany's mayor.

But for some reason, New York City called Ebby, though he

was broke and had no real prospects for employment in what was one of the nation's worst depression years. Whatever Ebby's reasons were for going to New York, the result would be his linking up with Bill—something that many AAs in the future would view as an act of providence.

Ebby described his experience this way:

> As time went on, I went to New York. I stayed with Shep C. for a while, and then I went to live with one of the brotherhood who ran Calvary Episcopal Mission on 23rd Street, near First Avenue [in] New York City." [In fact, the mission appears to have been near Second Avenue.]

Shep C., who also summered in Manchester, had an apartment in Manhattan and had even owned a seat on the New York Stock Exchange. He and Rowland undoubtedly knew of Calvary Mission as a result of their Oxford Group friendship with the Reverend Sam Shoemaker, who was then one of the most important leaders in the movement.

Shoemaker, a Princeton graduate and member of a prominent Maryland family, had found the Oxford Group as a result of a 1918 meeting with Frank Buchman in Beijing, China. Later he had been ordained as an Episcopal minister and was appointed pastor of Calvary Church in Manhattan's upper middle-class Gramercy Park area. One of Shoemaker's goals upon taking the pulpit at Calvary had been to establish a rescue mission in property the church owned in another section of lower Manhattan. This became Calvary Mission. It is likely that Shep and Rowland, who eventually served as a vestryman at Calvary Church, even handled the details in getting Ebby admitted to the facility.

In reviewing the conditions that finally brought Ebby and Bill together, the very existence of the mission should not be

overlooked as a key factor. It is surprising that Calvary Episcopal Church even had such a mission. While upscale churches
such as Calvary sometimes help *support* rescue missions, few
of them *operate* such facilities; this is left to the more evangelical sects and the Salvation Army.

Calvary Mission was actually an outgrowth of New York's famous Water Street Mission, founded in the last century by
Jerry McAuley, a mean drunk who had experienced religious
conversion in Sing Sing Prison. His idea of a rescue mission for
troubled indigents struck such a responsive chord in the community and had so much early success that New York's leading
citizens attended McAuley's funeral at his passing in 1884.

McAuley was succeeded at the Water Street Mission by S. H.
Hadley. His example of recovery from alcoholism was cited in
William James's *The Varieties of Religious Experience* (a semi-
nal book that profoundly influenced Bill Wilson). Hadley's son
Harry, who also had a religious conversion experience, was seek-
ing an opportunity to start a rescue mission when he met Sam
Shoemaker. The result of their collaboration was Calvary Mis-
sion, which helped thousands of men, including Ebby Thacher.

Ebby, likable as usual during his sober periods, fitted in well
at the mission and took part in their services and work. It appears that he was part of "the brotherhood," twelve men who
ran the mission and helped other indigents who came in for
short stays. Men who came there also made their personal surrender. Ebby's surrender date was given as November 1, 1934,
about a month before he called on Bill.

AA members believe that Ebby's more important surrender occurred in the cellar in Manchester, when he abruptly decided
not to drink the ale stashed there.

Since Oxford Groupers actively sought individuals who needed their help, it was not surprising that Ebby recalled his old Manchester friend:

> It was while I was staying there and working with the Oxford Group that I heard of Bill's difficulty due to drinking, and I phoned one day and got Lois, his wife, on the phone and she invited me over to dinner a night or two later.

According to information Ebby supplied in his subsequent AA talks, he had learned about Bill's troubles after visiting friends on Wall Street. Though broke and living in a rescue mission, Ebby still knew people in the financial district and dropped in to see them.

His account of actually contacting Bill varies slightly from Bill's own story, as he had said nothing about Ebby's earlier call to Lois. But it's possible that Bill either forgot about it or Lois hadn't told him of Ebby's call and preferred to keep it that way until Ebby talked with Bill in person. As Ebby would point out later, he was sober at the time, while Bill was drunk! In any case, the contact was made, and Ebby appeared at Bill's doorstep.

Ebby's later recollection about their meeting agreed with Bill's:

> While I was talking to Bill that evening, naturally he was impressed by the fact that I was sober and when I told him the reasons coming from the teachings of the Oxford Group, he, too, was impressed.

Bill walked to the subway station with Ebby and even said that "whatever it was that Ebby had found," he wanted it. Ebby found this encouraging, because he had felt—even when calling Bill—that his old friend would accept it completely or reject it altogether.

Afterward came the events described in Chapter One, when Bill appeared at the mission in a drunken state with the Finnish fisherman named Alec. According to Bill, he needed all afternoon to reach the mission.

A somewhat different, though still consistent, story of his visit was prepared in 1962 by a man named Billy D., who was a resident of the mission at the time Bill came there. Here is his recollection as supplied in a letter to a man named Larry M., who also must have been a former resident of the mission.

On that day that Bill Wilson called at Calvary Mission, Spoons Costello was in the kitchen and more or less in charge, as I was out all afternoon . . .

He came in two or three times that afternoon, asking for Abbe [Ebby] Thacher. Spoons told me about him when I arrived about suppertime, which was at 5:00 P.M. each weekday. Spoons told me a tall fellow, wearing an expensive suit of clothes [According to Lois, Bill still had an excellent Brooks Brothers suit, despite being broke!], very drunk, accompanied by a down-and-out, came in and each time made too much noise for Spoons to permit him to stay. Spoons, at that time, was our cook.

I asked Spoons if he had told the fellow about the meeting each evening. He said he had. When the meeting started, Bill was downstairs in the chapel accompanied by Johnson [undoubtedly Alec the Finn], . . . who judging by his clothes had been on the bum for some time. John Geroldsek, one of the brothers who lived outside the mission, was on the platform and in charge of the meeting. If you remember, the brotherhood took turns at conducting the meetings, selecting the Bible lesson, the hymns, and then leading off with their own testimony. Geroldsek had just finished the Bible and started to witness when Bill got up from the audience or congregation and started down the aisle toward the platform.

Ebby: The Man Who Sponsored Bill W.

Tex [Francisco] was superintendent at that time; I was assistant superintendent. Abbe Thacher was not present. [Bill said Ebby was there, as he undoubtedly was.] If you remember, we only insisted that the brotherhood attend a minimum of four meetings each week. The meetings were held every night in the year.

When Bill started down the aisle, I was sitting in the rear with the brotherhood men who were present. You remember, we seated the new men on the right side of the hall. By new men, I mean those that had not been cleaned up. Since Bill was accompanied by Johnson, his pal, he was seated with the group on the right. I asked two of the brotherhood to go down and ask him to sit down. He shrugged them off and walked to the front of the room near the platform. Geroldsek was getting mad at the interruption. Geroldsek was a heavyset man and by trade, a house painter. I went down the aisle to the front and spoke to Bill. You know how tall he is. And how short I am. I asked him to sit down. He said, No he would not. He had been trying to say something in this place all day and no one was going to stop him now. Seeing I couldn't quiet him, I asked Geroldsek to sit down and let Wilson talk. I told Bill we usually had the witnessing from the platform first, then opened the meeting so that anyone could witness from the floor, but seeing he was determined, we would open the meeting right away and he could say what was on his mind. Bill told us he had been at Calvary Church the previous Sunday night and saw Abbe Thacher get up in the pulpit and give witness to the fact that with the help of God he had been sober for a number of months. . . . Bill said that if Abbe Thacher could get help here, he was sure he needed help and could get it at the mission also. When the invitation [to repent] was given at the close, Bill and Johnson went forward and knelt down. When they got up, I suggested that Johnson go upstairs, but since Bill looked prosperous in contrast to our usual mission customer, it was agreed that he go to Towns, where Thacher and others of the Group could talk to him.

Billy D.'s account was given nearly twenty-eight years after the event, so it's likely that some of the details were in error. But both his and Ebby's accounts, as well as Bill's, give a picture of the fierce struggle Bill had in trying to grasp what Ebby had found and put it to work in his own life.

Ebby's account picks up the story:

> It was some time before [Bill] sobered up in Towns Hospital, and then I followed him up and later on we had many talks together. As time went on, I did a lot of work in the mission with the men we took off the streets and also I did a considerable amount of work in and about New York City, with various individuals when I was sent by the Oxford Group.

Ebby's visits to Towns Hospital typified Oxford Group practices that in AA became known as sponsorship. Ebby was, in fact, well suited to the sponsorship role. Years later, according to Ebby's Texas sponsor Searcy W., Ebby was quite good in talking over problems with other patients at the Texas Clinic. And Bill always felt that he had received good sponsorship from Ebby, and their discussions at the hospital were helpful. As Bill later wrote in his personal story:

> My schoolmate visited me, and I fully acquainted him with my problems and deficiencies. We made a list of people I had hurt or toward whom I felt resentment. I expressed my entire willingness to approach these individuals, admitting my wrong. . . . My friend promised when these things were done I would enter upon a new relationship with my Creator; that I would have the elements of a way of living which answered all my problems.

From this, it can be seen that Ebby had a basic understanding of the Oxford Group principles, which he could pass on to Bill.

But when Bill told Ebby of his sensational spiritual experience, Ebby was not quite prepared for it. He had neither seen bright lights nor stood on a mountaintop.

Ebby did, however, bring Bill a book that offered further explanations for Bill's enlightenment. It was *The Varieties of Religious Experience.* Ebby had not read the book himself, but Oxford Group members had recommended it. Ebby said that some of his Oxford Group friends thought the book to be a fine explanation of religious conversions.

In the case histories the book cited, Bill would find three common denominators. As related in Bill's biography, *Pass It On,* these three common points were (a) calamity, or complete defeat in some vital area of life, (b) admission of defeat, and (c) appeal to a Higher Power for help.

Bill, in reflecting on the book's case histories, could place himself within this framework. With the help of Dr. Silkworth at Towns Hospital, he had accepted defeat and the hopelessness of his condition. Then he had made his appeal to a Higher Power and had an amazing spiritual experience as a result of it. But why did he have a hope of surviving when countless other hopeless alcoholics before him had deteriorated, gone mad,

---

William James's *The Varieties of Religious Experience* has been called the source of the Alcoholics Anonymous program. This is not true; yet, it is a fact that Bill Wilson found in it important inspiration and ideas that were highly useful to him in developing the program. First published in 1902, this study by "the father of American psychology" is one of the most important books ever produced on the role of religion in dealing with human problems. Bill would refer to it continually in future years.

---

and finally died? That hope, he believed, came from Ebby. In 1954, he said:

> The difference between these cases and my own was not hard to see. The difference lay in my relation to my friend Ebby, himself a onetime hopeless alcoholic. As a fellow sufferer he could, and did, identify with me as no other person could. As a recent dweller in the strange world of alcoholism he could, in memory, reenter it and stand by me in the cave where I was. Everybody else had to stand on the outside looking in. But he could enter, take me by the hand, and confidently lead me out.
>
> On his first approach he was the bearer of bad news, but also of good news. The bad news was that I couldn't recover on my own resources, and that was a bitter, humiliating dose. But he had proved it out of his own experience, and out of the experience of alcoholics everywhere. He clinched this point, too, by telling me what Dr. Jung, the man of science, had said to Rowland.

While this message had shattered Bill's confidence in bringing about his own recovery, it had also made him ready for the gift of release, he recalled.

> One alcoholic had been talking to another as none other could. [Ebby] had made me ready for the gift of release. He had then held his own gift up for me to see. He was the living proof of all he claimed. Nothing theoretical or second hand about this.

Bill's Towns Hospital experience—though nobody could have discerned it at the time—had started something that would someday become Alcoholics Anonymous. According to his recollections, the concept of a helping society came to him even before his discharge from the hospital on December 18, 1934.

71

> While I lay in the hospital the thought came that there
> were thousands of hopeless alcoholics who might be glad to
> have what had been so freely given me. Perhaps I could
> help some of them. They in turn might work with others.

Bill did not have to look far for opportunities to help others.
These were already in place at both Calvary Mission and Calvary Church, and Ebby had set the example for him. Bill Wilson
returned to his home at 182 Clinton Street, though Ebby lived at
the mission for about a year before joining Bill and Lois there.

Ebby lived with them for about a year and also took part in
Bill's enthusiastic work with alcoholics at Calvary Mission.
Ebby apparently had occasional employment or received assistance from his family, because Lois recorded payments for
his board. He would eventually live with the Wilsons for about
three years when all of his stays with them were totaled up. It's
doubtful that he ever made more than a few token payments
for his board. During his sober periods, however, he was probably helpful and later on, after the Wilsons had established their
permanent home at "Stepping Stones," in Bedford Hills, New
York, he even served at times in a sort of house-sitting capacity
while they were away.

Ebby never grasped the Oxford Group message to the extent that Bill did, but he would have been involved in Bill's
work with alcoholics from Calvary Mission. He also accompanied Bill and Lois to the meetings at Calvary House.

There was a considerable difference between Calvary House

The Wilsons also had as another guest the Finnish fisherman,
Alec. Alec would have some drunken episodes while staying at
the Wilsons' and would then disappear completely, which Lois
would recall with some sorrow.

---

and Calvary Mission. Calvary House, next to Calvary Episcopal Church in the Fourth Avenue Gramercy Park area, was a seven-story structure that included the apartments for the pastors, rooms for guests, and a great hall for special meetings. Calvary Mission, located in a less affluent neighborbood at least a half-mile east of the church, was an old building adapted for the purposes of a rescue mission. Homeless men like Ebby sought refuge at Calvary Mission, while Calvary House and Calvary Church had at least a middle-class constituency. On some occasions, men from Calvary Mission were invited to the church to give testimonials about their conversions, but they were not likely to be involved as members at Calvary Church.

Ebby left no personal recollection of the Calvary House meetings. But Bill was deeply impressed, according to his 1954 recorded memories:

> On the platform and off, men and women, old and young, told how their lives had been transformed by the confession of their sins and restitution for harms done, dependence upon God for his guidance in all things. Travelers came from abroad reporting how God had claimed one country after another.

He went on to describe it as a movement in which social, political, religious, and racial lines seemed almost nonexistent.

> Little was heard of theology, but we heard plenty of absolute honesty, absolute purity, absolute unselfishness, and absolute love. Confession, restitution and direct guidance of God underlined every conversation. They were talking about morality and spirituality, about God-centeredness versus self-centeredness; they were talking about personal conversion and the conversion of the whole world. Everybody, good and bad, needed changing, they said.

Ebby: The Man Who Sponsored Bill W.

There's little doubt that the Wilsons found considerable inspiration and fellowship at the Calvary House meetings, though they were soon to encounter rejection and disappointment. Trouble came for a most unexpected reason: The Oxford Groupers were at first boundless in their praise of Bill as a recovered alcoholic. But they soon began to look upon this as being secondary to their main purpose of changing the world. The Oxford Group and its leaders had a message that was helping alcoholics like Ebby and Bill, but there were other needs of more importance, in their view.

It was also one thing to meet recovering alcoholics like Bill and Ebby, and something entirely different to deal with ripe drunks who were still drinking. As Bill recalled:

> It soon appeared the Oxford Groupers weren't too much interested in drunks as such. Just before Lois and I appeared, the Groupers had lodged several alcoholics in the upstairs bedrooms of Calvary House—the more respectable type of alcoholic coming from the well-to-do family. These hadn't done any better or as well as the boys at the Mission. When one, in a moment of alcoholic petulance had cast his shoe out of his bedroom, across the alley and into a fine stained-glass window of Calvary Church, the Oxford [Group] figured that they'd better stick to their mission of changing the world, and leave the drunks until later.

Bill and Ebby continued to work with residents at Calvary Mission, but this came to be seen as a separate activity that brought disapproval from the staff at Calvary Church. The Wilsons invited the mission residents to meetings at their Clinton Street home, and for a time things seemed to go well. Lois recorded in her memoirs how great it was to watch the change in the people who came to their meetings. But though the new fellowship had been strongly influenced by the Oxford Group, she noted that early incidents indicated that the two movements were not on the same course.

Bill and the Reverend Sam Shoemaker were good friends, she said, but one of Sam's assistants did not approve of Bill's working only with alcoholics and holding meetings in their home, away from the church influence.

> In an informal talk the assistant gave at a Sunday Oxford Group gathering, he made a reference to special meetings "held surreptitiously behind Mrs. Jones's barn." The atmosphere of the group from then on became slightly chilly toward us.

But perhaps the worst blow for Bill and Ebby came toward the end of 1935, when the leaders of Calvary Mission ordered the alcoholics living there not to attend the Clinton Street meetings. They said that the Wilsons were "not maximum," an Oxford Group term for people believed to be lagging or deficient in their devotion to the Group principles. "This not only hurt us, but left us disappointed in the group's leadership," Lois said.

It is well documented in Bill's writings and biography that the Oxford Group and Calvary Church leadership began to criticize him for what they viewed as his too-narrow focus on alcoholism when there was a need to deal with so many other world questions. He and Lois left the Oxford Group in 1937.

Sam Shoemaker parted with the Oxford Group soon afterward and formed his own movement called "Faith at Work."

The band of alcoholics that formed in Akron, Ohio, around the leadership of Dr. Bob retained their Oxford Group ties until 1939.

He and Bill continued to be good friends, and many years later Shoemaker even apologized for the rejection and criticism Bill had received at Calvary Church.

This early difficulty with the very people who had helped them was hard for the Wilsons, but it may have prepared Bill for the rocky times he would encounter as AA began to develop and grow. It must have been a confusing experience for Ebby too, particularly when the mission residents were forbidden to join him at the Clinton Street meetings. He continued to stay sober, however, and in 1935 and early 1936 he was a firm ally of Bill's as the early fellowship formed in the New York area. But personal troubles lay directly ahead.

8

The Lost Years

Ebby's sobriety had begun in 1934 just after his appearance before Judge G. in Bennington. Something had started working for him when he returned home and found that he couldn't drink the ale he had stashed there. He had promised the judge he would return sober. This promise, it turned out, lasted for well over two years. But he was about to begin a pattern of living that would include periods of sobriety followed by relapses, which AA members call "slips."

In 1954, he described his experience this way:

> I returned to Albany in the summer of 1936. After casting about for a time, I secured a job with the Ford Motor Company in Green Island, which is a town on the Hudson about ten miles from Albany. This was in the fall of 1936, November. I stayed with this Ford Company until the last part of April 1937, went on a trip to New York, and I fell off the wagon. That was after two years and approximately seven months of sobriety and work with the Oxford Group. I returned to Albany, and the old merry-go-round started, and I was drinking heavily and continuously for a long time.

If Ebby had his dates correct in this account, he must have found his initial sobriety in late August or early September 1934. Bill Wilson said that Ebby had had two months' sobriety before making that first all-important visit to the Wilsons'

Brooklyn home. But it's likely that Bill was in error, as he sometimes was on other calculations about specific dates.

Ebby's slip must have been shattering news for Bill and the tiny band of alcoholics struggling to stay sober in this early period. Though Bill had emerged as the prime mover of the group and was already dreaming of future growth, Ebby obviously had a starring role as the man who had sponsored Bill. In returning to drinking, Ebby became one of the first to embark on a pattern of living that is all too familiar in AA, a pattern that combines periods of sobriety with frequent slips. It would go on and on for the period between 1937 and 1953.

What was happening in Ebby's life that caused sobriety to lose its luster for him? It is well established that he was a person who suffered from nameless fears and frequent periods of depression. But thousands of AAs have similar problems without returning to drinking. He was also bedeviled by regrets and resentments. But this is also a common problem for recovering alcoholics who continue to stay sober.

A possible clue to Ebby's initial slip is that he might have considered himself as "being on the wagon," an expression that would not be used in AA because it implies a temporary venture into dry living that will eventually be replaced by drinking. Even in 1954, he referred to his slip as a sort of an accident when he said, "I fell off the wagon."

There also seem to be indications that Ebby had what might be called a "conditional view" of sobriety. His friends, including the Wilsons, thought that he believed he needed to find the right woman and the ideal job to stay sober. AA members who stay sober learn not to demand such terms: Sobriety must be preserved at all costs even if one is never able to find the "right partner" or the "perfect job."

Despite these problems, Ebby continued to work with the

Oxford Group after returning to Albany, and he also sought to help other alcoholics. He called on one man who never found sobriety. But years later, Ebby learned that the man's wife, though not admitting to alcoholism at the time, had learned something from Ebby's visit about her own problem and eventually got sober!

What seems remarkable is how Ebby was able to land in job opportunities that could have helped him realize his dreams. Getting a job in the inspection department at Ford was actually a lucky break in a time when thousands of people in the Albany area were out of work or on government assistance programs. But he might not have been happy in the job, and he later referred to a "straw boss" who gave him a hard time when Ebby returned to work after drinking.

Ebby had also drifted into a bad emotional state just before he drank again. As Ebby explained it many years later, he had been full of tension when he went down to New York City to have dinner with a woman friend. She always had a drink when they dined, he said, and this time he did too. By midnight he was roaring drunk and had to be dumped into a hotel. Despite being absent for several days without notifying his employer, he was permitted to return to work at the Ford plant. Perhaps as punishment, he was assigned a tough job unloading some steel from a railroad car. This became an excuse to drink again, and he lost his job.

With this difficulty, Ebby now embarked on another pattern that would continue all his life. This would be a pattern of relying on various AA friends to get him out of trouble and give him a place to live. While the Wilsons were the first to do this for Ebby, a pioneering AA member named Fitzhugh M. would soon offer his friendship in this way.

According to Ebby, he had an enjoyable stay at Fitz's home.

Ebby: The Man Who Sponsored Bill W.

In 1938, I came down and spent some time with Bill and during my visit, Fitzhugh M. from Maryland came also to visit Bill and he suggested that I return to Cumberstone, Maryland, where he lived, and spend some time with him, and we could have a good time together working around the place, where Fitz had done most of his drinking. So I went down and met his wife, daughters, and son. He and Bill were moving about the country a great deal, the idea of the book [*Alcoholics Anonymous*] was beginning to bud, and I was left with the family there and I would drive the youngest daughter, seven years old and stricken with diabetes. I would take her swimming and watch her and I had a very lovely summer.

This was another of Ebby's fine qualities, a love of children and an ability to relate to them. His niece, Ellen FitzPatrick, remembered his visits when she was very young. She and her brother, Ken, Jr., loved Ebby. He had a special way of twisting his hand just over her head and at the same time making a strange squeaking noise that delighted her; she actually thought his twisting motion was creating the squeaking sound. "When my daughters were little, he did the same trick with them, and they enjoyed it," Ellen recalled. Years later, while staying at a ranch near Ozona, Texas, Ebby would become like a favorite uncle to the family's sixteen-year-old daughter, Jan. Now nearly sixty, Jan still remembers how wonderful his visit was for her and her parents. Ebby was also a crossword puzzle expert, and he helped her improve her vocabulary.

Fitz M., who lived in the general area of Washington, D.C., was the early AA member whose story has appeared in all editions of the Big Book as "Our Southern Friend."

80

Ebby stayed with Fitz's family in the summer of 1938, when the country was still locked in a deep economic depression. Conditions were tough everywhere, but Ebby remembered it as a lovely period in his life. There's little doubt that the Fitz M. family also had warm memories of Ebby's stay with them. He could feel secure when he had no responsibility as a bread-winner, and many people liked to have him around when he was sober. He was charming and helpful. It's likely that the children in Fitz's family even adored him.

But Ebby's lovely times could be of short duration:

> Returning to New York that fall, I, of course, reached for the bottle again and was soon in trouble and somebody heard of a place in New Jersey called the Keswick Colony of Mercy for drunkards. I went over there, I think it was after the Armistice Day, and spent the winter. I returned to New York in the spring [1939], and through connections of my brother I secured a job at the New York State World's Fair Commission at the fairgrounds.

During that period, Ebby either was staying with the Wilsons or saw them frequently. Lois thought he was sober at the time and even attended meetings while he was working at the fair. "He could sometimes give us passes to one or two of the shows," she wrote in her memoirs. "It was great fun to be able to take friends from out of town to the fair occasionally."

Ebby didn't, however, claim sobriety for this period.

> I did not sober up. I managed to drink and hold it suffi-ciently well, and with so many people there, and crowds, I wasn't noticed much. I got away with it all summer until the fair closed in the fall, and I started up with some old cronies in Brooklyn, drinking it up pretty hard.
>
> Then in the spring I went to see my boss, who was

Senator Bennington's secretary, and convinced her that I was again on the straight and narrow and would she give me back my job? I held that and fell off again that summer, and in the fall, I again went to this place in New Jersey and spent the winter there. We worked outdoors and I got in shape physically but was not happy, although this was a fundamental, religious work there.

Ebby, in this summary, shows what his life had become. He had obviously sought the help of his older brother, the politically influential Jack Thacher II, in getting a job for which there would have been many applicants. He was apparently able to fool his superiors and associates, partly because of the nature of the work at the World's Fair. In convincing the senator's secretary that he was doing well, he was using the same kind of charm and persuasion that he would also employ in getting small handouts from the secretaries at the New York Intergroup and the AA General Service Office. There was something about Ebby that induced people to want to help him, though some of the help would be of the kind that is now called "enabling" in the alcoholism field. In the meantime, Bill and the fledgling society of Alcoholics Anonymous were finally completing the actions that would position AA as a national institution. The Big Book had been published, local publicity had produced lightning growth in Cleveland, and AA was developing in a number of cities throughout the country.

Though sometimes employed, Ebby spent two winters at the Keswick Colony of Mercy. Any records of this facility have been difficult to find, but one letter from Ebby to Ruth Hock must have been mailed from there. The address is given as Keswick Grove, New Jersey, a small village about forty miles north of Atlantic City. Ruth, who soon married and moved to the Marietta, Ohio, area, was the highly efficient young woman who managed the New York General Service Office in its earliest years. Attractive and friendly, she may have triggered Ebby's romantic interest, because he seemed anxious to impress her:

> I fear that you have gathered a wrong impression of my outlook on life but mayhap you were entitled to it judging from my eccentric behavior. No, a life with plenty of money and liquor has hardly ever been my sole aim—but what I was driving at was the cycle of about four months when I simply get fed up with myself and *whammo*. That's what I meant and I still wouldn't guarantee anything. After my flop following the initial spiritual lift and long sobriety I've never been able to regain the same feeling. . . .
>
> [Ebby had previously described the feeling that came to him after he decided not to drink the ale following his first court appearance in Bennington. He seems to have believed later on that he needed that *same* feeling to *regain* sobriety! He also notes here that he is caught in some kind of four-month cycle that condemns him to drink again.]
>
> Well, here we are, feeling much better in spite of a cold and several teeth that have been raising Hell. I've been shoveling the food in and I really believe I've almost got my stomach relined. Wonderful weather but I still don't like the scrub pines and sand of New Jersey appeasement: this part of N.J. at least. . . .
>
> In re to AA clientele besides Tommy there is present one Ted P. who graced Joy Farm [later called High Watch Farm] with his presence in company with Jack C., Bill, Sybil R. et al. He told me he didn't do so well but is still interested in AA. He seems pretty good people to me and we have had some good talks. There is some discussion of AA here among we inmates but have heard nothing from the powers that be. The latter have treated me swell.
>
> Slightly handicapped on account of lack of clothes but can't figure much out yet whereby I can get the things I

want in Brooklyn. Nor can I figure yet, not only the wise thing to do but the right thing to do for the best of all concerned as near as it's possible. Work not too hard yet. I'm pretty soft. I was lifting logs the third day but I didn't have what it takes—and haven't yet.

A good gang here—14 or 15 from the Carolinas—they sort of dominate. One from Brooklyn who knows all my Fulton Bar & Grill playmates though I never happened to know him. The rest scattered N.J., Penn. etc.

What is doing in New York and environs? You might give me any information you have concerning any AA activities in the sovereign states of the Carolinas and more specifically in the city of Richmond, Va. This for the use of the Solid South 10 well entrenched yeah [here].

Relax for a moment, light a Chesterfield, push aside stern duty, and pen me a few lines, and if you think of it stick a stub pen point in the envelope—this one is terrible.

My best to Bill, to Loraine, the better and bigger business for the book, and the work.

What really comes through in the letter is any lack of real discussion of the AA program, although he refers to it. He has been associated with AA but does not seem to be in it, and there is even a hint that he would like to be back at the Fulton Bar and Grill! But he always had acquaintances somewhere, both in and out of AA.

In the early 1940s, AA's growth in other cities gave Ebby an expanded network of friends. His first move was to Pennsylvania.

In June 1940, I decided that I would try my luck in Philadelphia and I went there. Somebody drove me down who happened to be going to town that day. I arrived there about ten o'clock, and by noon I was on the way to another drunk. Of course, AA had been established in Philadelphia by that time and I contacted them but they didn't—it was the old jealousy between New York and Philadelphia—they didn't seem to take to me. Anyway, I kept after them and they put me in the Philadelphia General Hospital in the psycho ward.

This recollection, made in 1954, was typical of the view Ebby sometimes had of his experiences. Going to Philadelphia, he had immediately gotten drunk and then felt victimized when the AA members there seemed cool to his call for help. To him, this was due to some kind of jealousy between New York and Philadelphia rather than the Philadelphia members' suspicion that Ebby might be a person who didn't really want to stay sober and perhaps wanted to use the group simply to bail him out of a bad situation. It's important to remember, too, that the entire AA membership in Philadelphia was then about seventy-five persons, which meant that their ability to respond to calls was also limited. Whatever the initial reaction of the Philadelphia members, however, he obviously prevailed and managed to be admitted to a hospital, presumably for detox treatment.

Ebby did leave the hospital with good intentions and soon found employment in a facility that helped homeless men:

When I got out, I went to live in a mission that had a truck service whereby they picked up newspapers, clothes, furniture, etc., much on the order of The Salvation Army, although this was merely a local establishment. I worked there about six weeks and secured a job with a hospital in Philadelphia as a porter in the cancer laboratory research division. I worked there about three months. In the meantime, I had made application to the U.S. Navy for a job as an inspector. This was after Pearl Harbor. They sent me a notice that my marks had been considerably improved, and I followed this up and soon secured a position as associate inspector of naval materials and placed in charge of a plant manufacturing torpedo parts and other necessary appurtenances for the Navy.

The time following the United States' entry into World War II has to be recorded as a good period in Ebby's life, with continuous sobriety for a long stretch. He undoubtedly took an interest in his work and did a good job. He was involved in work that was essential to the war effort at a time when patriotic feelings were running high. The work for the navy would have given him pride of accomplishment and a feeling that he was doing something worthwhile. Though Ebby was a single man, he was, at forty-six, too old to be drafted or even to be considered for military service. But working as a civilian for the navy was rewarding. It included a higher pay scale than on other jobs he'd held recently. At this time, in fact, Ebby was probably earning more than Bill, who was struggling to build interest in AA and had lived in poverty for several years.

But if interesting work was helping Ebby stay sober, it soon palled after it no longer seemed a challenge. Like painting the family home back in Manchester, the job was no longer satisfying once he had mastered it. "After a year or so, we had that pretty well licked," he said of the navy assignment. "Most of it was delivered and I began to lose interest and I got on a binge and the navy was mighty decent to me. They sent a couple of men over and said, 'Get yourself a good drunk and get it over with. We know your record, you haven't had a drink. You've done a good job.' But I couldn't make the grade, though. They finally gave me a release without prejudice."

In government service, a "release without prejudice" meant that Ebby could be rehired at a later time or in another federal job. It speaks well for his work record that his superiors tried to keep him on the payroll even when his drinking was giving them serious trouble. Their willingness to release him without stigmatizing him for future employment indicates that they must have liked him in spite of his troubles with alcohol. Ebby never worked again in a government job, but this wartime service with the navy was clearly an opportunity for lifetime employment with a good pension that he lost through drinking.

Despite losing his navy job, Ebby had no trouble finding new employment. His next position also suggests that it was a real opportunity for growth. "I next secured a job with a local contractor who was crating trucks for shipment overseas and I worked up to assistant purchasing agent."

Ebby, in working for the family business in Albany, had been listed as purchasing agent. He may have had an aptitude for this type of work. During World War II, such a position would have been both challenging and interesting, requiring a person who was good on the telephone as well as resourceful in tracking down supply sources and expediting delivery of scarce materials. Ebby should have been well suited to this job. But it didn't last, nor did others that followed.

I got drunk on that job. And I had several other jobs. I worked in Westinghouse in the steam turbine division in South Philadelphia. I worked for the Red Cross in a packing depot where we were packing stuff to send to the American prisoners in German and Japanese prison camps. Then I had a couple of hitches as steward of the AA Club on South 36th Street, on the campus of Pennsylvania University.

But things were bad. I'd have a couple of months on the wagon and six months off and so on until the fall of 1945. I decided to return to New York. I lived with Bill and Lois Wilson, and for a time I worked in the circulation department of the *AA Grapevine*. I went along all right until I again fell off the wagon and then I was sent to Kent, Connecticut, [to] High Watch Farm.

High Watch, still in operation today, would see a great deal of Ebby. Originally called Joy Farm, it had been founded by a gracious woman named Sister Francis, who virtually turned it over to AA after learning about the fellowship. At the time Ebby arrived there, a man named Johnny Supple was in charge. Supple would take Ebby under his wing, but their future relationship would turn out to be stormy at times, and Ebby's return bouts with the bottle would not help.

Yet things started well at High Watch.

Johnny Supple, who was mighty good, asked me to be his assistant as he had to do a lot of traveling. I was there the summer of 1946 and the summer of 1947. Later on I joined

---

Lyn H., a graduate student at Vanderbilt University, has written a scholarly paper about High Watch and prepared excerpts from some of Ebby's correspondence on file there. The letters reveal much about Ebby's behavior and attitudes during the 1946–47 period. On May 2, 1946, Ebby's oldest brother George scolded Ebby: "It has been your history to date that, whenever you got a little money ahead you immediately gave in to your ego and [did] not get back to any sort of normal existence until you were both broke and physically down and out." At the same time, however, George was offering to set Ebby up in some sort of pen distribution business, and two of his other brothers, Ken and Jack, both wrote to Ebby urging him to accept George's offer.

Johnny in Dublin, New Hampshire, at an AA place up there called Beech Hill Farm.

During his stay at High Watch, Ebby kept in touch with his oldest brother, George, who owned a stoker-manufacturing firm in Massachusetts.

On November 7, 1946, George wrote to express surprise upon receiving a letter from Ebby and to learn of "the shabby way" Supple treated him at High Watch Farm. While the details of this so-called shabby treatment are not known, Bill Wilson believed that Ebby had actually been the one to give Supple a difficult time, at both High Watch and Beech Hill. Ebby was then back staying with the Wilsons. George wrote two weeks later on November 21 to say, "In my opinion Bill and Lois have been extremely patient and more than kind to you and I surely hope you fully appreciate and will repay them by your actions in the future."

George seemed genuinely interested in helping Ebby, but his letters show that he felt Ebby was responsible for his own troubles. On January 7, 1947, he told Ebby:

> You complain that nobody in AA seems to be able or want to help you get a job. . . . Granting that you are the victim of a very dread disease, you have many times been cured to the stage where you could have gone on and up.

Perhaps feeling this was a bit harsh, George wrote three days later to say:

> It has occurred to me that perhaps the field in which you have had the most experience is in commissary work. You did run the AA's club house in Philadelphia; also you did have charge for several periods of the Farm in Connecticut, so why don't you look for something in this line.

Ebby: The Man Who Sponsored Bill W.

On January 17, 1947, George was clearly upset with Ebby, who had recently received some money from Jack and was presumed to be out drinking. George wrote:

> When you will get this letter I do not know, probably not for some time in view of the fact that almost as soon as you had obtained funds by borrowing from Jack you started back on the road to oblivion. . . . I have been listening to the talks over the radio on the problem of the alcoholic and have gained from the various discussions by doctors, psychiatrists, lawyers and laymen that no alcoholic may be helped who will not help him or her self.

Ebby was apparently back at High Watch when he received the following letter, dated March 23, 1947, from a woman in New York named Mary H., which shows the consternation of one who liked him but wondered about the curious pattern of his life:

> Friday night at 39th St. Bill told the story of your helping him. Told it simply and humbly and said, "When my friend Ebby left me," etc. The man he was talking about was a great guy and it was you. That guy stayed sober a long time and sounded peaceful and happy. Where is he, Ebby? Under what is he buried? What is between him and his faith in God? Do you remember saying once to me that when you let any thing come between you and your faith in God you lost that thing? Well, Ebb, maybe that's what happened with AA. The organization of AA became too important to you—you let it come between you and Him—did you, Ebb? Well, maybe you'll say that [I am] crazy but if you could have heard Bill Friday you would realize why I have to write and say that the guy who gave that message to us drunks should be the happiest guy in the world. I for one am hoping and praying that this time you have gotten back that faith and that you will be the happiest guy on earth.

Ebby also received critical letters from other relatives. The following, dated March 27, 1947, is from George's wife, Grace, sent from their home in Melrose, Massachusetts:

> In my return to the house last night I found your letter which gave me in varied degrees, a surprise, pleasure, and a taste of disgust.
>
> The surprise came from the postmark on the envelope, the pleasure, of course, from hearing direct of you, and the taste of disgust at the fact you do not think or write openly and contritely of the real reason for your being back at High Watch Farm. From reliable sources I have learned that ever since January when you borrowed $125 from Jack you have been on and off the wagon continuously. How could you or anyone expect to earn a living or of accomplishing anything living that way. Then I have heard that a friend of Wilson's, one Robert A. Shaw connected with the Church of the Neighbor in Brooklyn, has been kind enough to interest himself in you and to give you aid and shelter. In all probability, I am only guessing now, he and Wilson have been instrumental in again placing you at Cornwall Bridge.

Grace was quite preachy in the letter but did concede that Ebby's condition was physical and then advised him to devote himself to helping others.

> But as I read your letter this thought is far from your mind and you are again concerned with the petty and material affairs of your surroundings and the bickerings and by-plays of your associates, with the thought still deep in your mind that you have been persecuted and discriminated against by others, while the real facts might well be that it is your own ego that is at fault.

Such scolding must have hurt Ebby's feelings, but many of his friends and relatives would make similar comments in their letters. While he had occasionally done well at High Watch, this did not keep him sober, as he freely admitted.

Rock Bottom

Ebby, during his lost years in the New York area, still kept up his contacts with family members. His brother Jack had stepped down in 1940 after fourteen years as Albany's mayor and was now in private law practice. A high achiever, he would also be a judge and a bank president and was, of course, the brother Ebby always looked to for help.

Jack expressed his concerns to Bill in a November 12, 1948, letter:

> I have just heard from Edwin [Ebby], who tells me that he is temporarily employed by the Fenimore Riding Camps, with a School of Horsemanship at 242 East 20th Street, New York, N.Y., and that he needs some clothes and also a pair of shoes, shirts, etc.
>
> I am sending two suits of clothes to him today and I am enclosing a check for $50.00, which I am relying upon you to see will be used for the purposes for which he has asked.
>
> I am glad to learn, at least, that he is doing something to help himself but was not very much impressed by what he said to me insofar as his future is concerned.
>
> Will you write to me, as soon as possible, and let me know what the situation really is, and whether you feel that New York is the proper place for him?
>
> Albany is not, because of his many failures here, and

Philadelphia is in the same category, and I do not know
what confidence those who know him in New York have in
his ability to straighten himself out.

A smaller community might possibly offer him a greater
opportunity.

Will you let him know what I have said because I prefer
to wait two or three days before I write him myself?

Bill apparently brought Jack up to date on Ebby's activities and
kept the fifty dollars for what he hoped would be Ebby's neces-
sities. On December 9, Jack wrote to Ebby, whose address was
shown as 137 Seventeenth Street in New York. Jack had received a telegram from a friend suggesting that he make an
investigation of Ebby's activities. Jack wrote to Ebby:

I do not know what you have been doing since you commu-
nicated with me two or three weeks ago, but imagine that
you have slipped back to your old ways.

Therefore, I want you to understand very thoroughly
that so long as you prefer this course in life I can do nothing
for you nor will I send money to you now or at any time in
the future while you are drinking.

I have asked Bill Wilson to keep in touch with me and let
me know what and how you are doing. Therefore if I hear
from him that you are making an honest and sincere effort
to rehabilitate yourself I shall be glad to do what I can to assist you, as I always have in the past. However, you must
qualify by your own conduct and effort and desire to be
a man.

Jack finished by commenting that he had to pay for another
family member's surgery and that he did not intend to throw
money Ebby's way to use for the wrong purposes.

Bill, who received a copy of the letter, replied immediately.
His long letter to Jack dated December 14, 1948, disclosed that

Ebby was, indeed, going through a very rough patch with his drinking:

> Have just received the copy of your letter to Edwin [Ebby], and most reluctantly, I've again been driven to the same conclusion as yours.
>
> At the beginning of this last cycle we got a job for Ebby at a riding academy owned by a woman who also has a summer place in the mountains. If things went well in the winter there would have been a later project of his becoming manager of the summer place.
>
> All went well for two weeks. I advanced Eb $20 of your $50 to get him caught up. Then came trouble and the job was lost. Pending finding something else he was allowed to use his room at the riding school. Meanwhile I rustled him a job (with a sanitarium in our town) which would be available in a week. He pulled himself together and came up to see us Monday following Thanksgiving. He looked so fit that I mistakenly advanced him $20 more to tide over to the new hospital job.
>
> Again things went bad—very. He appeared at the riding school and gave the woman owner a pretty rugged time. Scared, she moved him to a rooming-house nearby and got in touch with me, continuing, however, to supply him with meals at a restaurant. He also phoned me and though not too enthusiastic about the hospital position, thought he would wait to take it, being, as he was, financed in a room and food for the time intervening. To take up this slack I sent the riding school lady your last $10 and a little more— whereupon Eb promptly disappeared for several days. Finally he phoned me about the hospital job, but I felt obliged to tell him that under the circumstances I couldn't urge the hospital to take him in. I felt it would be useless, that he would have to stay sober for a considerable period before I could be persuaded to go any further.
>
> The sad fact is such, that the poor boy has become

completely irresponsible. He has been in New York this time about three years, one of them spent with Lois and me, the result, saving brief intervals, has always been the same. As you so well know this leaves me in a terrible quandary. If you don't finance him you think you may be letting him down, when actual experience fairly shouts that one is actually hastening his destruction.

Considering what he did for me years ago, it's a heartbreaking situation, for which I seem to have no answer at all. It may be that a six-month commitment to a State Hospital could give him a chance to pull together for a fresh start. But this he doesn't want; I'm sure he'd resist it bitterly. Being perfectly sane when well sobered up, he'd be out on a threat of habeas in 10 days.

So Jack, I can't think of a thing to do, but wait the while, resolutely refusing him money to drink. For that is all that a job or money means to him at present. While I have by no means given up hope of his ultimate recovery, I do feel there is not a single thing I can do about it now.

Have you any suggestions?

In reading Bill's letter, it is easy to see that he wavered from his strongly held beliefs about alcoholism when Ebby was the person under consideration. By late 1948 Alcoholics Anonymous had about seventy thousand members and vast experience with the problems of recovery. It was well understood in the fellowship that patching up a person's difficulties while he is still drinking might only delay his eventual recovery. Bill says as much when he talks about "hastening his destruction." Yet he could hardly ever resist making one more effort in the hope that it would work this time.

Jack replied three days later, on December 17:

I am in the same position that you are with regards to Edwin. This last experience convinces me that it is impossible to send him money for any purpose whatsoever, as he uses it only for the one thing.

However, with Christmas coming on, I have been disturbed to think that he would be alone in New York without a room possible, or the money to obtain meals. I feel that he has become completely irresponsible and will remain so unless he gets some medical attention.

I do not feel that he needs a private room, but I am of the opinion that a medical check-up and a stay in the hospital for two weeks might make him able to think things out more clearly. In the event that this meets with your approval, will you let me know and tell me how much it will cost.

In the meantime, if you have any knowledge of it, I would appreciate information as to his whereabouts.

Bill was aware of his own tendency to give Ebby special treatment and he thought other AA members did so too. Bill mentioned this problem in his reply to Jack, on December 27:

Thanks for your latest suggestion about Edwin.

I saw him the day before Christmas. He was fairly sober, though just off a heavy one, I am afraid. He wanted money, which by a great effort, I refrained from giving him. This occurred at a meeting where I imagine he did succeed with some of the others. The dickens of it is, Jack, that so many of us feel under such obligations and gratitude that we continue to do this, though we know quite well he will drink it up.

About your offer of two weeks hospitalization, it's very hard to advise. His general health appears to be fair despite the drinking. He does not seem to suffer the ungodly hangovers that most of us do. I am very much afraid that two weeks at a hospital or one of our farms would only bring the same result it has so many times before; it would just get the poor boy in a little better shape to drink again.

Perhaps his best chance would be in a three to six

months voluntary commitment with a job waiting when he got out. That might give him a real chance to get cleared up and freshly started. The State places around here aren't bad at all; hundreds of the local AAs have been in them. Maybe it could be arranged that he get some special psychiatric attention at such a place. This is a course that has never been much tried. But would he do this?

Bill was clearly grasping at straws in suggesting a voluntary commitment in a state hospital as something that might give Ebby "a real chance to get cleared up and freshly started." Everybody had run out of ways to help Ebby. Neither Bill nor any of the New York AA members knew how to help him. It was not entirely gratitude that caused members to respond to Ebby's pleas for money. Ebby was likable and knew how to ingratiate himself with people. He had perfected these skills out of necessity, for how else could he have survived with frequent drinking and little employment?

Ebby would also find repeated chances for sobriety. Following the frantic period in late 1948 when Bill and Jack were discussing what was to be done, Ebby received an opportunity to join Johnny Supple at Beech Hill Farm. Beech Hill had recently been established as "a mountaintop rest home for recovering alcoholics in Dublin, N.H." Johnny had gone through stormy times with Ebby at High Watch, and Ebby had even accused Johnny of unfair treatment. But the Beech Hill opportunity called for a new start—and Johnny may have entertained the hope that he would get Ebby Thacher on the right track at last.

Giving Ebby employment at Beech Hill was almost the equivalent of offering a person an ongoing vacation with pay at a lovely resort. Beech Hill under Supple's direction was such a promising facility that Bill Wilson even took steps in 1951 to secure Dr. Silkworth a sort of retirement medical position there. Silkworth, who had treated Bill years earlier at Towns Hospital and wrote "The Doctor's Opinion" for the Big Book, was then seventy-eight and, as Bill put it, "must soon give up his labors at Towns and Knickerbocker Hospitals . . . and so wishes to retire to the country . . . there to continue his work with alcoholics." But Silkworth died of a heart attack a few months later, before he had a chance to move to Beech Hill.

Beech Hill, which is still in operation, opened in what *New York Times* reporter John W. Stevens described as a sprawling, frame, turn-of-the-century manor house atop Beech Mountain (as it was then known)—1,800 feet above Dublin pond and 1,365 feet below the apex of nearby Mount Monadnock. "A single-lane, unpaved cowpath—featuring three hairpin turns—linked the 79-acre woodland site with the village below." It was also described as having a family atmosphere—guests could play croquet and go swimming in the Hill's spacious outdoor pool. It was the sort of place that would have appealed to Ebby and should have evoked pleasant memories of his childhood summers in Vermont.

Ebby did spend time as Johnny's assistant at Beech Hill. It didn't last, as Bill explained in an April 21, 1950, letter to Emma D. of Upper Darby, Pennsylvania:

> The news on Ebbie is this—he stays sober three to five months at a time. Then comes that gradual emotional build-up you know so well and he falls down again. Each time we think that he is going to make it and then, poor devil, he doesn't. In the last three of these cycles much of his sober time has been spent with Johnny Supple, who had the Farm at Kent, Connecticut, and who now has a place at Dublin, New Hampshire. On each try Johnny has attempted to make him his Assistant Manager. But poor Ebbie fell off again only a month ago and now I fear Johnny

is pretty discouraged. At the moment our poor friend is back in New York where he receives some help from Twelfth Step House, and is living at the Municipal Lodging Place. Any number of people have tried to help, mostly with money, but they all eventually make the sad discovery that money only means liquor. It is pretty rugged on Lois and me, and the rest of us. But what can one do?

Ebby, in 1954, had this recollection of the period following his time at Beech Hill.

On returning to New York, of course, it was the usual pattern all over again from the start. I did get a job for a time with an export company, run by an AA man and I held out there for a while, but I hit it up again. So finally, I went to a place in Katonah, Westchester County, which was only about three miles from Bill Wilson's home in Bedford Hills, and there I worked. In the winter I helped paint the farm, get it ready for the next year, and worked when we could, weather permitting, and in the spring I helped them plant corn, potatoes, and hoed, cultivated the produce as it came up.

Physical labor did seem to work well for Ebby, at least for a time, and even his recollections hint that he was proud of these intervals when he was out in the open exerting himself. Since he was working only a few miles from Bill and Lois, his association with them would also have helped him maintain short-term sobriety.

His next move was to become an orderly in an asylum.

I left there to take a job in a hospital in Rye, New York, a mental hospital and I didn't last out there. So I hit New York again, and immediately, right on the old Third Avenue pattern.

The people who remember Ebby from those years can supply brief vignettes of a man who was often never completely sober, but still knew enough to make his way around the city. Eve M., a General Service secretary from 1951 to 1968, had previously worked in the New York Intergroup office.

Eve remembered Ebby coming into the office. On one occasion, looking down from her second-floor vantage, she saw him going down the street, walking with one foot on the curb and another in the gutter, bobbing as he walked but still comfortable enough not to change the situation. There were also times, she recalled, when new AA members sought to become the people who would finally help Ebby find sobriety. But it never worked.

Nell Wing, the nonalcoholic woman who served as Bill Wilson's secretary for many years and later became the AA archivist, remembered that on one of his drunks, Ebby stumbled into the reception room at the General Service Office and passed out on the couch. He had done this several times. In any other office in New York, this would have been reason to call the police, but the GSO staff members were reluctant to take such actions, especially with Ebby.

Nell said that while they were wondering what to do with Ebby, a well-dressed, scholarly appearing man arrived. "He said he was going to write a book about AA, had done a lot of research, but lacked a vital piece of information," Nell

---

From her second-floor desk by a window, Eve M. could look out on the street and recalls, with pleasure, an AA bus driver who always waved as he drove past, making the brief encounter "sort of a small AA meeting."

---

recalled. "Could I tell him what happened to Ebby T., who had brought the Oxford Group message to Bill Wilson?"

The coincidence was a shocker, and for a moment Nell wondered what to say as she looked first at the visitor and then at the slumbering Ebby. "I confess I found the moment too dramatic to pass up. So I just silently pointed over to the couch and quickly showed him into Bobbie's office [who was an early General Service secretary]!" she said. "I don't know if he ever finished the book or not!"

Nell described Ebby as intelligent, charming, and articulate when sober. "But drunk—that was something else again," she recalled. "His main objective then was to hit us up for a half-dollar or a buck, and though it was a policy not to give him money, we all did...." But she did recall many interesting conversations with Ebby during his sober days.

Lib S., one of the earliest General Service secretaries and now a retiree living in North Carolina, remembered Ebby as a perfectly awful drunk who would make himself a nuisance so you'd give him money to drink. But she did not want to remember Ebby that way. She added in a soft voice that "Ebby was a channel in God's work."

Lois Wilson, in her own biography, *Lois Remembers,* referred to Ebby's life as an erratic career:

> Periods of sobriety mixed with long periods of maudlin drunkenness. It was hard to know how to handle him when he came begging for money, for we all felt so deeply in his debt that we hated to refuse him.

Nobody felt this dilemma more keenly than Bill Wilson. In working with Ebby, Bill appeared to forget everything that he and AA had learned about alcoholism through bitter experience. Yev G., a member of the Manhattan group since 1941,

thought that Bill lost all perspective when Ebby went off on another drunk. Yev recalled in 1980:

> Bill was so definitely concerned about Ebby and so fond of
> him and felt so grateful and indebted to him that he would
> do anything, rather than have anything happen to Ebby.
> Some of us were Bill's selected emissaries to go out and find
> Ebby when he went out on one of his episodes. We knew his
> watering holes, the rooming houses, and the places where
> he went. So we'd get him back and bring him back in the
> group, and he'd go along very well. But we had to observe,
> really, that Bill did not treat Ebby with the same kind of ap-
> proach that he realistically would with the average kind of
> alcoholic member we had in the small groups we had in
> those days in New York.

Yev even thought Bill was an "enabler" for Ebby. Bill was so
grateful to Ebby, Yev said, that he was incapable of giving his
friend the "tough love" that alcoholics sometimes need if they
are to recover from their disease.

Ebby, relying on help from Bill and AA friends, continued to
survive in New York, but haphazardly. Some of the time, nobody knew where he was. By the early fifties, however, AA was
growing rapidly throughout North America and was already
reaching into many foreign countries. It's likely that many AA
members—sober residents of the New York area or visitors to
the city—sometimes saw Ebby but thought he was a vagrant
roaming the sidewalks of Manhattan, looking for a handout for
a drink, a meal, or a night's lodging. His appearance would
have been wretched. At times he would have been drunk or
badly hung over.

Nobody but Bill and a small group of friends knew that this
homeless man with the unsightly appearance had once taken
an action that led to the recovery of thousands. But now he

was a person who badly needed help himself. Given his appearance and condition, however, some would have viewed him as beyond help.

But as 1953 unfolded, a new opportunity lay just over the horizon. Ebby Thacher, who had failed in several states, was about to get another chance in a place he had never considered: Dallas, Texas.

10

A Time of Renewal in Texas

In 1953, nearly two decades after he'd carried the message of hope to Bill Wilson, Ebby was himself nearing a point of complete collapse. His whereabouts were sometimes a mystery to his AA friends. Now nearly fifty-eight years old, he was starting to live on what could easily be called borrowed time. It was sober up or die. The odds were that it would be "die."

But now a chain of events intervened, much like the series of encounters that had led him to the Oxford Group and Bill. He would be offered a new opportunity in Texas that would at least give him some of the happiest years of his adult life.

He would also find status and recognition among some of the most generous AA members in the country. It really was true, in Ebby's case, that Texas was a big state with a big heart. And he would say years later that he would have died if he'd stayed in New York.

Several key people were involved in what was virtually a conspiracy to take Ebby to the Dallas–Ft. Worth area. In Texas were Searcy W. and Olin ("Olie") L., both early AA members with a strong devotion to the program. In New York were Bill Wilson and Charlie M. And, surprisingly, there was also a role for Cebra G., one of the three Oxford Group members who had called on Ebby in Manchester in 1934. Cebra had moved to France, but he still had ties to members in the program.

Searcy W., who celebrated fifty-one years of continuous sobriety on May 10, 1997, had created the reason behind Ebby's move to Texas. Searcy took his last drink in 1946 at a sobering-up place in Dallas. He soon went to work with the Yale Summer School of Alcohol Studies, at the insistence of the legendary Dr. Elvin M. Jellinek, and an AA member named Horace F. Searcy recalled:

> I was told by the good Dr. Jellinek that even if I knew what was wrong with me, I'd still have to take the same treatment, that being Alcoholics Anonymous.
>
> I then established the Texas Clinic-Hospital for Alcoholism on Fairmount Street in Dallas in 1950. This was because there was no way any general hospital would want to treat drunks. There was still no medical help for the alcoholic. Then, over a period of 18 months, because AAs all over the country would take patients directly to AA from the Clinic, we treated over 700 patients. All of them who would go to AA stayed sober because of following the AA program.

In early 1953, Bill and Lois finally came to Dallas in response to repeated invitations from Searcy, who had previously visited them at Stepping Stones. After escorting Bill on a tour of the clinic one morning, Searcy posed a question for him: "After all of these years of this miraculous recovery we are all making, what would you rather see happening in AA now?"

After an early setback in Texas, Ebby would enjoy nearly seven years of continuous sobriety and would hold the same job for several years—an incredible achievement in view of his previous work record.

Bill's immediate reply, according to Searcy, was, "I would like for Ebby to have a chance to sober up in your clinic."

It was only a wishful comment, but Searcy immediately accepted it as Marching Orders from On High. He made reservations for Ebby at the clinic. It was a case of acting on faith alone, because Ebby was nowhere to be found. There was also still the problem of getting him to Texas and into the clinic.

That assignment fell to Charlie M., an AA member who had moved from Texas to New York after finding sobriety. Here's how Ebby himself recalled in 1954 the events that took him to Texas:

> I was wandering around New York and I used to drop in at the [New York] Intergroup office; it was then at 28th and Lexington Avenue, and I must admit it, I looked for a handout. [I was] trying to get enough to get a few drinks [so] I could get in a place and cadge a few more.

He was greeted by Hazel R., who later worked for AA General Service as one of the corresponding secretaries. As Nell Wing later explained, Bill and others advised the women in the AA office not to give Ebby money, but they usually did! It's not known if Hazel was a soft touch for giving Ebby money, but she is remembered as an unusually kind and loving person.

Ebby continued:

> Hazel R., bless her, came over and said, "You know, I think I've got something for you. Charlie M. has been over in Paris, France, and he ran into one of your friends from the Oxford Group who came to see you originally."

At a small AA meeting in Paris, Charlie had met Cebra, who had joined Shep C. and Rowland H. in helping Ebby during the summer of 1934. "They talked it over," Ebby said, "Cebra asked how I was, and Charlie said he'd heard not so good and Cebra said, 'Let's see if we can't do something for him.' Charlie got the hunch that I ought to come [to] Texas."

Why did Charlie M. develop such a special interest in Ebby? As Nell Wing recalled, Charlie shared the goal of many AA members in New York—to be the person who finally helped Ebby Thacher regain sobriety. There was considerable regret that the man who had sponsored Bill was continuing to suffer. People wanted to help him recover what had been so freely given to others.

Hazel R., already knowing of Bill's and Charlie's interest in the Texas Clinic, immediately called Charlie to tell him that Ebby was in the office. Charlie quickly said, "Hold him there until five o'clock and I'll be down!"

Charlie, surely to Ebby's surprise, took him to Ebby's favorite bar for a "doubleheader" and ordered a soft beverage for himself. By this time, Ebby had to be wondering what Charlie had in mind. AA members were usually kind to Ebby, but kindness didn't include buying drinks to support his habit!

After Ebby had settled in with his drink, Charlie dropped his bombshell: "Ebby, how would you like to go to Texas?"

Ebby was shocked. "My God, who wants to go to Texas?" he exclaimed. "They've got no water down there, the cattle are dying all over the place, I don't want to go to Texas. I'm broke, I haven't a cent to my name, and I have no clothes."

Charlie, apparently a good salesman, explained that it might be a good idea to get Ebby out of New York. He even suggested that some of those Texas ranchers down there might take Ebby in and give him some opportunities to work on a ranch. In any case, life in Texas had to be better than what was happening with Ebby in New York. He asked Ebby to think it over and gave him a five-dollar bill.

Ebby, speaking years later before an AA audience in San Jose, California, painted a grim picture of the condition he had been in that day. The only redeeming thing was that he had learned how to use the five dollars so he'd at least have a bed that night. He did that by saving a dollar, which in 1953 provided 75 cents for a cheap room and 25 extra cents—to get him into a bar the next morning where he could mooch some more drinks! In the meantime, the remaining four dollars could support an evening's drinking.

He had apparently learned to budget in this cunning way because he was so sick of being out in the cold weather in New York all night and riding a subway (for shelter) and being arrested and spending ten days in jail at Riker's Island. He also recalled that it was not pleasant to walk around the streets in the slush all night long. He said he used to walk from Fourteenth Street to Seventy-Second and back again, completing three or four round-trips to make a night.

That meeting with Charlie was on a Thursday, Ebby said. On the following afternoon, he met Charlie again and got another five-dollar bill. This time, Charlie said, "I'm not going to come around to see you anymore, but the offer still holds."

Ebby, despite his continued drinking, must have reviewed his options and decided that Charlie's proposal made sense. So on Saturday he went to see Charlie and agreed to go to Texas. Charlie got him a clean shirt, let him take a hot shower, and threw away his old underwear. Then Charlie telephoned Olie and Searcy in Texas.

Although Charlie was holding the telephone, Ebby could hear Olie's booming voice roaring out of the receiver: "All right, send the Yankee son-of-a-bitch down here!" Despite his condition, Ebby must have wondered what he was getting into by going to Texas.

So, on Sunday, September 6, I boarded a plane, arriving in Dallas that evening. I was met by Searcy W. and Olie L., two men who proved to be great friends.

But Ebby's first several weeks in Dallas were hardly a happy time. Searcy noted that Ebby arrived aboard an American Airlines flight "with all his earthly possessions in an old Pan Am tote bag, with a pint of whiskey. We met him at Love Field in Dallas, where there was no problem spotting him because he looked the part."

Olie L., writing to Bill Wilson sometime later, said Ebby "was in pretty rough shape" when he arrived. He was placed immediately in Searcy's Texas Clinic, Olie said, adding: "A slight improvement was shown during the first week and we were elated. Then, for about a month, he was the most uncommunicative, cantankerous son-of-a-bitch you have ever seen. All he could do was grunt like a goddamn hog, and then, he got worse."

That was the bad news. Fortunately, there was more to the story. Ollie continued:

Now for the bright side of this episode. About a week ago he started clearing up and talking to people. His complexion is clear and pink—his eyes are bright. He has started laughing and talking of going to work. . . . Saturday night he was in full bloom and fine fettle at our annual party given in your honor. . . .

We have sorta dressed him up and he looks good. He has got a few things on his mind such as a few old debts, a little tax problem and a few things of that nature which will be rectified as soon as we can secure proper amounts, names and addresses.

In other words, Bill, today, November 9, 1953, I feel that Ebby has more than an even chance of recovery. His remarks concerning you are measured, deliberate, and with love, and of course I have reason to believe that this is a considerable change.

Olie added, "Much, much credit regarding Ebby's present well being should be given Searcy and his staff at the Clinic. They have exhibited patience and tolerance beyond description, and all without pay." As a final note on the typed page, Olie scrawled, "Old Ebby acts like a man who wants to get well."

Bill replied on November 17, thanking Olie profusely and calling his letter "the best damn news I've heard in years." He went on to say that despite "all our discouragements here, I somehow have a strong confidence I can't really explain that Ebby is going to see daylight at long last. God knows, nothing would make me more happy."

During those first weeks at the Texas Clinic, Ebby said he was in a fog. According to Searcy, it was days before anyone, including the nurses, could give him medication, but with glucose, vitamins, intravenous medications, and withdrawal of alcohol, Ebby had auditory hallucinations. At one point he even thought opera music was coming from the air conditioner. At the end of six weeks Ebby was no better, Searcy said, and he told the head nurse to get him ready for his return airline trip to New York. But she replied that she could see some improvement in him.

"I listened in disbelief," Searcy said, "but in a few weeks Ebby was walking, talking and wanted to go to the AA Club. Thus, Ebby went to AA. After two more weeks he went with me to Lubbock and talked some at an open meeting. He continued to recover."

This marked the beginning of an unusual sojourn for Ebby—a Texas interval of eight years that would include moments of joy and hope. In New York, he had been just another vagrant on the streets, shuffling along Third Avenue and

scheming his way into cheap saloons and flophouses. But in
Texas, he became a celebrity of sorts almost from the start, be-
cause, as he put it, "people wanted . . . to see the guy who
couldn't sober himself up but . . . did sober Bill Wilson up."
Word quickly got around that he was a patient at the Texas
Clinic. AA members even wanted to visit him there.

Ebby's presence in Dallas would also bring another important benefit for Texas AA members: a visit by Bill. The Ninth
Annual State AA Conference was scheduled for June 11–13,
1954, in nearby Fort Worth. The conference committee members were hopeful that Bill might agree to be the main speaker.
Inviting Bill would have been a long shot for most state confer-
ences, because even by 1954 Bill was receiving so many speaking invitations that he would have been on the road
continuously to honor them. So he had adopted a policy of declining all such invitations unless there was a special reason
for visiting the area or making the talk. (In 1951, for example,
he had made a whirlwind speaking tour of major cities to win
acceptance for the adoption of the General Service Conference. But this was done for what he considered a purpose essential for AA's unity and survival.)

In April 1954, he made an exception to his "no-speaking"
rule and telephoned conference chairman Jack H. to say that
he would come to Fort Worth in June. The reason? It was to
express his gratitude for the help Ebby was receiving in Texas.
As Bill explained in a May 10 letter to Jack:

> The thought of what you have done for Ebby scarcely
> leaves my mind for a day. It is, of course, on that ground
> that I am creating the excuse to visit Texas. Word of my
> visit is already getting around and already the invitations
> are pouring in from other areas and groups. They all say in
> effect, "If you can go to Texas, why can't you come to us?"

and I shall cite my desire to see Ebby and convey my appreciation of what you have done for him and the generosity of Texas in general as a special reason for coming to you.

Making such a travel decision in early 1954 could not have been easy for Bill, because it had been a rocky time for him. Lois had been ill, requiring surgery, and was only beginning to recover. His father had died in Vancouver, Canada. His death reactivated the sense of loss that Bill had felt as a nine year old when his parents had separated and he didn't see his father again for another nine years. Also in 1954, Yale University offered him an honorary doctorate, which he finally declined (for the good of AA) only after much soul-searching.

In the meantime, Ebby was still living at the Texas Clinic and was beginning to make new friends in the Dallas area. One of them was E. D. "Icky" S., an older member and chairman of the Northeast Texas Committee for the General Service Conference. At one point during his recovery at the clinic, Ebby had gone walking. In his confusion he had been picked up by the police, who suspected him of being a member of a car-theft gang. Though he was sober, his confused mental state resulted in his being taken into custody. Icky got him out of jail and thus became both a friend and a protector who would stand by Ebby throughout his stay in Texas.

Icky, writing to Bill on February 18, 1954, noted that he and Ebby had been friends ever since the day "I got him out of jail down here." Icky described Ebby as the original owner of "being lonely." He said, "Ebby thinks he needs a harem of good-looking young rich girls and they are all taken up. Time will tell how well he can recover as he has been mighty sick at heart." Icky went on to say God had helped him and "I know that God will help Ebby."

But according to Ebby's January 1954 letter to Bill, life was getting better for him. A woman named Betty was planning to help him write his life story. He was also in the process of getting a securities dealer's license. Though he was still living at the clinic, he was showing signs of becoming more independent. Searcy was spending a lot of time with him. They would sometimes meet with other friends in Searcy's home for gabfests that would last until early in the morning.

The June state conference in Fort Worth included a wonderful time of reunion for Bill and Ebby. They were photographed together, and Bill made a special effort to record Ebby's recollections of his own life, his drinking history, and the events leading to his 1934 meeting with Bill. At the conference, Bill had the opportunity to chat with others who were trying to assist Ebby. Ebby was asked to deliver a short talk at the conference. He commented on how well he had been treated and explained how his move to Texas had come about, an action he clearly believed was much more than coincidence. From his remarks, it was clear that he wanted to stay in Texas forever. Though most AAs tend to dismiss "geographical cures," his was apparently working!

But what was he to do for a living? Bill was hopeful that Ebby would be able to establish himself in a suitable type of business. He outlined this in a July 27, 1954, letter to Russ R. in Laguna Beach, California. Russ had been one of the early band of alcoholics who lived with the Wilsons at 182 Clinton Street in Brooklyn when Bill was trying to jump-start the movement in New York:

> In spite of the crowds, I managed to see quite a little of Ebby at Fort Worth, later at Dallas. He has been doing a lot of speaking at meetings and shows more signs of really joining AA than ever before. While it may be that in part he is doing this in the ancient hope of finding the right girl and

the right job, I do think it has a constructive component which one can't doubt. The Texas folks are about to finance him as an agent for a new sort of garbage can—something on which one of our AAs in Michigan has the national distribution. The can itself is a steel cylinder, two feet across and two feet deep which is sunk in the earth. This is surmounted by a conical top with a cover on it. You dump garbage onto the ground beneath. Then you dump in some bacteria that chaw the garbage. Apparently, they mostly liquify it and it runs off. It takes two years to fill the thing up and the residue is a good mulch. Nationally, they are selling three thousand of these things a week, so it is a proposition that really looks like a possibility. They are willing to finance Ebby to the extent of loaning him a car and buying his first lot of cans. I hope it does give him a start, for the job business has been almost as uncertain as before. As to the girl—well, I don't know. That is indeed in the lap of the gods!

While Ebby apparently never thought much of this garbage-can idea, Bill's letter does reveal his own enthusiasm for entrepreneurial business ventures, an interest that would continue throughout his life. It is also likely that Bill had felt that Ebby could perform this type of selling if he really tried. But nothing came of it. And Searcy, though he felt Ebby had many good qualities, didn't believe Ebby was cut out to be a salesman dealing with the public.

While Ebby's future employment was still up in the air, he received an invitation to a Texas ranch. This recalled Charlie M.'s suggestion, made the previous September, that "some of those ranchers down there" might give him an opportunity. In the summer of 1954, shortly after the Texas conference, he spent about two months at the Triangle-J Ranch near Ozona, Texas, with Ralph and Mary Lee J.

Mary Lee, an Alanon member who was widowed in 1972 and is now herself deceased, recalled Ebby's summer visit to their ranch. Mary Lee and her husband, Ralph, had met Ebby at the Fort Worth state conference. They liked him so much that they invited him down to their ranch in the rolling, live oak country between Ozona and Sonora. About a month after the conference, Olie L. brought him down, Mary Lee said.

Ebby stayed with them almost two months. Mary Lee and Ralph were so fond of him that he could have stayed much longer. "We had many wonderful days with Ebby," Mary Lee recalled in 1981. "We would get up early in the morning, and would always have breakfast. He enjoyed it because we always had three meals a day, family style."

Ranch life agreed with Ebby. Mary Lee couldn't remember if he knew how to ride horseback when he came. At first they kidded him because he held the reins too tightly and forced his mount's head back. But he could wear Ralph's work and riding clothes, and before long he was helping Ralph with the roundups and other ranch work, even the sheepshearing. They also spent lots of time in the pool or simply riding horseback through the hills. "All I can think of is a pleasant summer with Ebby," Mary Lee recalled.

The J. family, of course, was seeing Ebby at his best.

The J. family raised Aberdeen Angus cattle, Rambouillet sheep, and Angora goats on their seven-thousand-acre ranch, which Mary Lee described as "small" by Texas standards. They also had bountiful pecan trees, and Mary Lee made pecan pies that would melt in the mouth. She recalled that Ebby liked his eggs "just so" in the mornings, but he worried about being spoiled because they also had steak for breakfast.

Though he would visit them again in 1958, they never saw the unpleasant side that his other friends had seen while he was drinking. Ebby did regale them with stories of his earlier drinking days and even told them of selling his parents' furniture to buy whiskey (which may explain why there had been so little furniture left in the Thacher family home in Manchester in 1934). Other AA members drove out to the ranch to meet Ebby that summer; the Texas people were clearly proud to have with them "the man who carried the message to Bill Wilson."

On August 6, about midway through his visit to the ranch, Ebby sent a decidedly upbeat letter to Olie. He described some of his activities at the ranch in humorous terms and even told how he hunted doves on the ranch with a twenty-gauge shotgun. In bagging one with his first shot, he called it "beginner's luck I guess for I haven't fired a gun in twenty years." Whether he remembered it or not, this must have been almost exactly twenty years since he had blasted away at the pigeons while sitting on the lawn in Manchester!

In the same letter, Ebby mentioned Mary Lee and Ralph's daughter Jan and her steady boyfriend. Jan, now Mrs. Fred Van Shoubrouek, was a high school girl living at home during Ebby's visit to the ranch. She also has wonderful memories of him.

Jan remembers that Ebby occupied a back bedroom at the ranch with windows that provided excellent cross-ventilation. The swimming pool was actually a tank for the livestock, but it served very well, and they spent many hours there. She remembers Ebby as a cultured man with many interests.

But one issue was disturbing to her. In 1954, Jan still remembered the turmoil of her father's drinking, though Ralph was a Texas AA pioneer who had been sober for years. She was grateful for what the program had brought her family. She accepted the AA belief that alcoholics can never return to controlled drinking. She clearly recalls, even to this day, that Ebby did not accept that for himself. She says he really believed he could become a controlled drinker. They even had a few arguments about this issue while sitting around the pool.

By early September 1954, Ebby was getting ready to return to Dallas, though Mary Lee J. said they would have liked having him stay on at the ranch. She also remembered that she had to leave the ranch to attend to her ailing mother. In any case, Ebby seemed optimistic in this September 4 letter to Olie:

> Though I really believe the J.'s would like to have me stay, they are having a succession of guests starting next week, beside which it is time I get the Hell out of here anyway and get busy, so I am heading back to Dallas some day after Labor Day next week. The latter day reminds me of my arrival in Dallas last Sept. and all you and Searcy and many others did for me. How I will ever be able to repay all of you is a tough question but maybe I can get back at you in some small part. I have it always in mind and I am grateful.
>
> When I get to Dallas I shall have to find some employment as soon as possible. Ralph and I have tried to dig something out down here but no success. The time has come when I can't go on depending on you fellows to keep me going, you have all been swell, but it's not fair, and damned if I like it either. No more deals, thank you. While I am better physically, I have tried that type of work around the ranch and facts are facts—I just can't take it in the heat. I will have to get some sort of clerical or other light work that pays just enough to live on.
>
> Charley sent me a check for $25.00 and I am sending Mrs. Graham $16.00 which pays me up until Sept. 16. As you can see I shall hit Dallas with not much left. It will be necessary to ask someone to stake me for two weeks or so for the additional room rent and food, but that's all I ask. I'll have to find work in that time. I shall start plugging on my

own, but of course will appreciate any leads or suggestions any of you may offer.

A few days later, Ebby returned to Dallas, and also to the problem of finding employment. Earlier that year, he had referred to his efforts to become a securities dealer, but that hadn't turned out well. As he said in his July 1954 recording:

> Although I secured a job as a security salesman and it looked pretty good for a while, it petered out. I didn't have a car, couldn't get around, and I couldn't dig out the prospects. I couldn't stand the physical exertion of hitting those pavements every day. I suppose that's the penalty I have to pay for all the drinking I've done.

Ebby had another bout with drinking in late 1954, his last for about seven years. He then went to work for an AA member, Hal N., who ran a print shop. The pay was small, but Ebby stayed with it; it was, reportedly, the first job he ever quit sober.

It's not known why he quit the print shop. But he was apparently on good terms with his employer, who wanted Ebby's help in enlisting Bill in an oil-field investment idea.

It was an ambitious plan, one that seemed far beyond anything Ebby had previously attempted. Ebby and his employer seemed to assume that Bill had important friends who might be willing to invest in the proposition. They may have forgotten that Bill's friends on Wall Street had dropped him long ago and that his efforts to rejoin the financial world had come to nothing (though AAs would often say that his ill-starred business trip to Akron in 1935 was now paying handsome dividends!).

Here, in part, is how Ebby described the proposition, in an April 6, 1955, letter typed on the printing company's letterhead:

The other day, my boss, Mr. Hal N., who has met you by the way, called me into his office and outlined a plan he has on tap and last night took me out to dinner and we again went over his proposition.

Hal, with his partner, . . . has under lease slightly over 1000 acres of land in Okmulgee County in Oklahoma, some of which is not much over eight miles from the now famous Edna field, which is producing such phenomenal results in oil yield. There are many abandoned oil wells on Hal's property and most of these were drilled prior to 1920 at which time the industry had no known means of breaking up the tight sand formation to recover the oil reserve. Of late years a method has been developed which has given excellent results. This is a hydraulic fracture termed "fracking" in the industry, whereby a liquid combined with sand is forced under high pressure into the sand formation on all sides of the well, so breaking it up as to allow the oil to again permeate that it may be easily pumped out.

In a third paragraph, Ebby added names of a geologist and others who had expressed confidence in the likelihood that Hal's lease would undoubtedly be productive. In a fourth paragraph, he discussed the tax advantages, including the attractive oil depletion allowance that was available if the well turned out to be a producer. He went on to explain that Hal wanted to get a group together in New York to buy interest in the wells and would cut Ebby in on any wells he could raise money for. Ebby then asked Bill to read the letter carefully and to go over in his mind to see if he couldn't think up some people to get together and create some interest. "If so Hal will send me on East and very probably come along into the bargain."

Bill's reply, dated only six days later, showed that he had no wish to pursue the matter. He explained that his "acquaintance hereabouts is far less than it is with out of town AAs." He conceded that there were individuals around New York with considerable capital, but he didn't know any of them personally. He didn't feel he should seek out any who were total strangers. He also noted that it would not be in good taste if he were to use his AA influence, even on Ebby's behalf, with virtual strangers.

He then referred to the garbage-can business that had been proposed for Ebby the previous year. That was a little different, he said, because not a great deal of money was required, "so I had no hesitation in approaching people you already know in Texas on that score."

In Dallas, some of Ebby's affairs began to show improvement. He had found a room and was almost paying his own

---

In closing a letter to Ebby, Bill mentioned that things were rocking along in New York, "mostly in anticipation of the St. Louis affair," the upcoming Second International Convention of AA. "I think I wrote asking you to come up—all expenses paid. I do hope you can get away for the occasion. Obviously, there will never be another one like it."

This was certainly true: The July 1955 convention in St. Louis was a watershed event in AA, because it included, on July 3, turning over AA's Three Legacies—Recovery, Unity, and Service—to the movement. Attending the event, in addition to Ebby Thacher, were many others both in and out of AA who had contributed to the fellowship's origin and growth. Ebby attended and received special recognition, of course. Others among the seven thousand persons attending were AA pioneers from throughout North America and Europe, as well as friends such as Father Edward Dowling, the Reverend Sam Shoemaker, and Dr. Harry Tiebout.

---

way with a little help from others. His pay at the printing plant was only thirty-seven dollars a week, but he stayed with it and stayed sober. After he left the printing company, he worked for a time as a flagman for Icky, who was in the construction business. He then went to work for Ben T., an AA member who reclaimed old bricks.

But it turned out that reclaiming old bricks was grueling work for a man of nearly sixty. Even though Searcy said that Ebby was physically a well-built, strong person, the brick job was almost too much for him.

He was rescued from this ordeal by an AA member named Tom B., who said years later that he had thought the brick work was going to kill Ebby. Tom, who operated a surplus aircraft parts business at Love Field in Dallas, offered Ebby a job that included bookkeeping as well as managing the parts bins and inventory. The pay was higher than at the printing plant, and Ebby fitted in well at Tom's business. He stayed there a number of years—longer than any job he had ever held except the early employment at his family's firm in Albany.

Ebby's progress in managing his own affairs and staying sober won him considerable friendship and support in Dallas. More than ever, he now appeared to be an AA member taking personal responsibility and moving ahead in sobriety. Others saw this too. In a letter to Nell Wing dated August 20, 1981, an AA member from Florida named Marty P. shared her memories. She was living in the Dallas area when Ebby arrived there. She had witnessed the change in Ebby. She referred to the men who had helped Ebby get his start in Dallas:

> Then we all had the pleasure of watching the change that began in Ebby. Where he had been quiet and full of resentment and a loner he blossomed into a friendly, talkative, grateful, productive citizen of our town and group. He was

very proud of his job. He gained weight and seemed for some time to be healthy and happy. I know we were all so happy for him, as we all felt that some recognition for the part he had played in helping Bill was long overdue and neglected.

He was asked to speak at a number of groups in our vicinity. Also the men I mentioned saw to it in the beginning that he had clothes and an old car for transportation.

Yet, there were other members who saw Ebby differently, as never quite happy. Jean C., from Dallas, in an August 12, 1981, letter to Nell, described Ebby this way:

Ebby looked like the Dick Powell of the "thin man" movies. He was slender, lost, soulful eyes, and appeared depressed. Most of us felt sorry for him and he smiled rarely. But you could see that he had been a fine looking, small man.

Ebby was also in demand as a speaker at large AA meetings, although he didn't approach these assignments with a great deal of confidence. In the very beginning of his stay he had gone to Lubbock, Texas, and Roswell, New Mexico, with his Texas sponsor, Searcy. At later times he would give talks in Memphis, Tennessee, San Jose, California, and Davenport, Iowa, where he would join Searcy on the platform. His tapes reveal a speaking voice that was pleasant, with a deep quality that Nell Wing described as "gravelly."

For most of his stay in Dallas, Ebby lived in a rooming house at 3618 Gillespie Street. With Icky's help, he had bought

---

Ebby did resemble the famous William Powell who starred in the popular "Thin Man" movie series of the 1930s.

---

a car. Icky also let him use his credit card for gasoline and oil. Ebby had became a popular figure at the Suburban Club operated by AA members in the area. This may have been a sober version of the friendships he had once tried to find at sleazy bars in Manhattan and Brooklyn.

In the meantime, Ebby continued to hold a job—no small achievement for him. Tom B., his employer for many years, liked Ebby, but he was also somewhat critical of Ebby's attitude. "Ebby . . . was a peculiar duck," he said in 1981.

> He kind of thought the world owed him a living, to a certain extent. He thought he never got the recognition that he should. That was down in his craw for years. He stayed sober though, there with me, and did a very good job. I started him out at about $50 a week and he got up to about $90 when he was working for me.

This question is asked frequently: Did Ebby hold a resentment over a perceived lack of recognition, despite Bill Wilson's expressions of gratitude and efforts to include Ebby in important affairs such as the 1955 St. Louis convention?

One AA member who thought so was Bob D., a management consultant who was living in Malibu, California, when he wrote to Nell Wing on August 28, 1981. He had known Ebby during his Texas years, and said:

> It was . . . easy for me to determine that Ebby held a deep resentment for Bill, Dr. Bob, et al., because he felt he was more the founder of what became AA than anyone else. This could really account for his repeated "slips" in the program.

But if Bill was aware of such feelings on Ebby's part, he never took note of them or took issue with them. If Ebby had such feelings, he was not the only AA member to hold them. Bill had faced opposition and criticism from several early AAs in the Akron–Cleveland area. He had learned to dismiss them virtually without comment. He never lost sight of the contributions these other persons had made to AA's early growth, and he always acknowledged it even while being criticized. And even if such attacks hurt him deeply, he did not react by fighting back or by denouncing his critics. His letters and articles over the years clearly show that he felt it wise for individuals as well as the AA fellowship to avoid such pitfalls.

Lois was somewhat less forgiving of Ebby, though she went along with Bill in helping Ebby and even letting him stay for extended periods at Stepping Stones. In her biography, titled *Lois Remembers,* she discussed Ebby and his difficulty in keeping sober after initially carrying the Oxford Group message to Bill. One of her thoughts was that Bill had wanted sobriety with "his whole soul," while Ebby may have wanted it simply to keep out of trouble. "Or maybe he *couldn't* want it with his whole soul, because he was too ill," she suggested. She added, "Beyond that crucial visit with Bill, Ebby seemed to do very little about helping others. He never appeared really a member of AA. After his first slip many harmful thoughts seemed to take possession of him, and he appeared jealous of Bill and critical, even when sober, of both the Oxford Group and AA." She then conceded that she felt disloyal in writing this way about Ebby, "but it is important that future generations of AAs know why Ebby was never considered the founder of AA." She did acknowledge that Ebby died sober, and that he was always someone special in Bill's thinking.

But "special" is almost an understatement. Bill had served almost as Ebby's enabler during the troubled years leading to his departure for Texas. He continued to watch over Ebby like an elder brother. While "geographical cures" are frowned on in

AA, Bill thought that Ebby's relocation to Texas had been a good move, though largely because of unusual friends like Searcy, Olie, and Icky. They corresponded frequently.

Bill also sent Ebby money from time to time, sometimes in response to Ebby's requests. Ebby, although slowly getting pay increases at Tom B.'s company, never really supported himself completely, though he achieved far more independence in Texas than he had during his New York years.

In any case, Bill's continuous interest in helping Ebby was one of the wonders of AA. Marty M., one of AA's very first female members and also a key figure in the alcoholism movement, explained in a 1980 interview that few of the early New York area members recovered. "The only one that kept coming back was Ebby Thacher," she said, "and that was because Bill went fishing with a fishing net. He'd haul him in." She also went on to say that Bill's helping Ebby "was more than just gratitude. I think that he felt a kinship with Ebby. What kind of kinship? I don't know, but a very close one, brothers is as good as any." And like many others who knew Ebby, Marty described him as a very likable person and added, "I was one of those who worked on him, and knocked myself out trying to help him."

11

The "Perfect Woman"

Ebby had always believed that the right woman and the right job could bring him the happiness he wanted. While the job with Tom B. fell short of his grandiose dreams, he would say in his talks that he had given up on the "big shot stuff." The plan to make big money in the oil well recovery method was probably in that category, and Ebby must have dropped it after Bill showed no interest in becoming involved. But in working for Tom B., he was showing an ability to work conscientiously in an ordinary job and meet his responsibilities, as thousands of other AA members learn to do.

Then a woman came into his life. While this should have been a blessing, there were a number of Texas friends who thought she became instrumental in Ebby's downfall. But for a time the relationship did bring him a measure of happiness and fulfillment.

She was Chloe K., an attractive woman who had been an actress but was a nurse at Searcy's clinic when Ebby met her. Searcy had been forced to fire her, he said, because of her pill habit. Since Searcy sold the clinic in 1957, Ebby and Chloe must have started dating about that same year.

Ebby thought Chloe was the great love of his life. In 1958 they went to visit Ralph and Mary Lee J. "I think he really was in love with Chloe," Mary Lee said. "And he told Ralph, 'I had to live this long to fall in love.'"

Though Ebby was in love with Chloe, she may have looked to him for the support he could provide, limited as it was. And later on, as she became more seriously ill, Ebby even cared for her. This was an unusual role for Ebby, since others were usually looking out for him.

Tom B., his employer, thought that this kind of helping may have even been good for Ebby and helped him stay sober. "One day I figured it out," Tom said. "Ebby was always a taker, never a giver." But helping Chloe, Tom thought, was the first time in Ebby's life he tried to help somebody. "He became a giver."

This was a strong judgment that overlooked Ebby's helping mission when he carried the Oxford Group message to Bill Wilson and apparently shared with others during the fellowship's earliest months. But in his years after his 1937 slip, he had indeed been a "taker," moving from one situation to another in search of people who would look after him. So his romantic interest in Chloe as well as his devotion to her was a marked change for him.

But Chloe was ill. While this did not threaten Ebby's sobriety, he was pressed for money. Tom had raised his salary to about ninety dollars per week, but Ebby still wrote to Bill for "loans," which actually became gifts. Bill, in sending money to Ebby, would consistently express gratitude for the time Ebby had helped him. "This is a real opportunity to again set on the record my terrific gratitude for that historic call you made upon me in Clinton Street twenty-five years ago," Bill said to Ebby in a 1959 letter that accompanied a check for two hundred dollars. "The consequences to me and to so many have just been beyond calculation."

Earlier that year, Ebby had shared his concerns about Chloe in a letter to Bill:

Of course you know my friend Chloe has been a sick girl. While she hasn't had a drink in 2½ years—[she has] a complicated condition bordering on malnutrition, plus inordinate fears, plus change of life crisis—a pretty trying situation.

In 1960, Ebby again became Bill's special guest for the International Convention, this one in Long Beach, California. Ebby now had six years' sobriety and was again looked upon as a successful AA member. Life seemed to be good for him. His Texas friends could take considerable pride in the part they had played in taking him from the streets of New York to a fairly comfortable life in Dallas.

In 1961, however, trouble started to surface in what was really a fragile situation. While Ebby had finally found in Chloe the woman who would be the great love of his life, a good friend saw it differently and was deeply concerned. Icky S. had been Ebby's devoted friend almost from the beginning of Ebby's stay in Dallas. Now he was beginning to express real concern about the future. In a March 27, 1961, letter to Bill, Icky frankly stated that "Thacher does not have money trouble but has GIRLFRIEND trouble and does not earn enough money to take care of her and give her the things she demands of Ebby." He described Ebby as "a very lonesome man and this Gal friend lets him pick up all of the expenses and gives him the crumbs. She is a very sick person and Ebby has taken it upon himself to be the sole support and it is not healthy for either one of them because that cannot last."

Icky went on to say that Ebby was "very thin skinned morally and cannot ever break his set of laws and stay sober." He did not say that Ebby and Chloe were living together, though Searcy has said that they did. But it was clear in Icky's view that such an arrangement would violate Ebby's own code.

[I] think that he is one of the best men at heart [I] have ev[e]r known and he just cannot shack up with some gal and not be married. The gal is not going to marry him and cares nothing about him except what cash and prestige she gets out of him as one of the Founders of AA. She would not walk across the street for Ebby if it was not for what she can get out of him.

Then Icky added this general observation:

All women are of the same cloth when it comes to getting out of man what they desire.

Bill wisely refrained from commenting on Icky's final statement when he replied on April 6. The only reference to Chloe was that Ebby thought the association was keeping him sober and interested in going on living. "Therefore it's rather hard, as a bystander, to judge what is good for him," Bill said. "I suppose that's rather up to him."

The main part of the letter was about Ebby's current income problems. Bill also shared with Icky his concern about Ebby's future, when he could no longer work. He had discussed this with others at AA headquarters. There was the suggestion that Ebby be given something out of AA funds, although Bill was not sure about the precedent this would establish. But as noted in *Pass It On,* provision was made in 1961, at Bill's request, for Ebby to receive a regular monthly check for the rest of his life. The Trustees of the General Service Board agreed to send him one hundred dollars a month in the beginning, and something like two to three hundred dollars a month more, if he should really fall ill. This was an unusual decision, but Bill's influence with the trustees was so strong that they went along with most of his requests. Bill also went further by organizing a tax-free "Thacher Fund" made up of private donations. He invited friends to contribute on a one-shot basis.

Such actions showed how thoughtful Bill was in his planning for the future, because Ebby's situation was beginning to deteriorate in 1961. In a September 13 letter, Bill told one of their mutual friends (apparently from the old Oxford Group days) that Ebby had begun to get into really bad health. He had, Bill said, a deteriorating lung condition that kept shutting down his oxygen supply.

But the really devastating shock for Ebby was Chloe's death later that month. Bill, in a September 28 telegram, said:

> We are desolated with you at the loss of Chloe and we send the deepest sympathy and affection. Please phone collect . . . and tell us all about it. Charlie says you will be here Saturday. Why don't you come with us to Bedford Hills Saturday night after the meeting?

How did Ebby react to Chloe's death? According to his employer, Tom B., Ebby got drunk the very next day. If this recollection was accurate, then Ebby did indeed feel that his sobriety hinged on his relationship with Chloe. In any case, he drank again. Tom also felt that Ebby had a pill problem.

This created problems that were reflected in his work. Ebby began to make so many errors in his bookkeeping that the auditor mentioned it to Tom, who called Ebby in for a conference.

"Ebby, I feel kind of bad," Tom remembered saying to him. "An old friend of mine has got hooked on pills." When Ebby said, "Well, I don't know anything about pills," Tom's reply was direct: "Ebby, that old friend is you."

Ebby became indignant and denied that he was using pills. Later on, however, after he had returned to New York State, he wrote to Tom and apologized for his actions. Tom had reluctantly dismissed him, although he always said that Ebby had done a good job until "he got on pills."

Tom, who was also an AA member, made the additional observation that he never thought Ebby "bought the AA program 100 percent." Since Tom was closely associated with Ebby for a number of years, he had come to know him well and must have made this judgment as a result of things Ebby said and did. Yet he and the other employees at Tom's company liked Ebby. Tom remembered him as "a fellow with a twinkle in his eye."

With Chloe gone and himself now facing unemployment, Ebby could only feel that his future in Texas had suddenly grown bleak. He had also slipped. So he returned to the Texas Clinic for treatment, though it was no longer operated by his Texas sponsor, Searcy. At this point, it was likely that Bill urged Ebby's friend Icky to send him back to New York in December. This was slightly more than eight years since Charlie M. had whisked him aboard an American Airlines flight for Dallas. Ebby still had friends in Dallas, but it was Icky who bought his ticket and saw him off.

Bill wrote to Icky on December 28. He enclosed a check for $80.75, drawn from the Thacher Fund, to cover Ebby's fare. "Ebby arrived okay," Bill wrote. "He seemed fine—except for his much weakened state. And he was most grateful for what you and all the other folks down your way have done for him over the years, and recently. This will always be gratefully remembered by me also."

Ebby would live at four different places for the next 2½ years. For a time, he would stay with his brother Ken in Delmar, New York, an Albany suburb.

While at Ken's home, on July 30, 1962, he wrote to Ralph and Mary Lee J. in Texas. Excerpts from his letter show that he could still express himself well in writing to people who had been real friends:

Having met Chloe, I know you both understand why I liked her so much, and I must say she did much to keep me going—and so did your friendship. Although I flopped miserably I also had a long period of being sort of "puny" before that flop. Guess I wasn't as rugged as I should have been.

I smile at myself at my attempts at being a real tough hombre on a horse and I'll warrant Mary Lee had a laugh when she took me out that first time—believe me I am no caballero! I was better off in the pick-up the time we rounded up the sheep, though I did get a pretty good workout with old Ralph in the chutes. Pleasant memories.

Seems to me I sent you a post-card lately but don't recall what I said. I was with Lois & Bill W. for a few days, got into N.Y. City on two days and visited two AA clubs and found exactly 3 people whom I knew. Went on to Manchester, Vt., and spent one day wandering around by myself, Lois & Bill having gone to Burlington to visit a sick family member there. The next day Bill and I did ride around a bit looking up old spots. It was 50 yrs. ago this coming Fall we were in school together there. We did see a few old friends and acquaintances and in some instances we found they couldn't care less, but this is natural—after that length of time other people have also had a lot of this life, and their paths have been different. Then again in my case I was a pest at times, plenty of times. They did have an AA group there but it broke up, 3 former members still living in town and sober as far as I know, but I could not locate them, all were reported out of town for the week-end. So much for this.

When I left your ranch I weighed about 170, today about 122 but I've been getting my strength back and moving around more. Whether I have deserved it or not, the fact remains that much help, rest and good food have brought me a long way back to health—amen. Those vitamin injections are great stuff for awhile. They filled me so full of every known high power kind before I left Dallas, the effect lasted for more than a month, then as usual I had a let-down, and man what a slump I hit. But that's water over the dam.

As usual, too much "me" in this, but I wanted to bring you up to date, you would have possibly heard thru the grapevine, but sometimes that medium garbles things up a bit. Sure glad to learn that Jan and her husband are doing so well, it must be a source of real pride for both of you, I hope they continue well and busy. I know you both are doing that very thing. Ralph, you keep out of as many draws as possible. Heard that Dallas and vicinity had some recent heavy rain. How's the grass on the ranch?

You both take care of yourselves and please remember me to those I know when you meet them in your travels. One of the N.Y. gals said Ralph asked about me in Austin—I appreciate that.

In addition to staying at Ken's home, Ebby would reside with the Wilsons for almost a year. He would then be at Chit Chat in Pennsylvania and again at High Watch in Connecticut, where he had once worked with high hopes of being the manager. For two years, he would also have difficulties with drinking.

In October 1963 he was Bill's guest at the annual dinner given for Bill at the Hotel Commodore in New York City. As always, he was introduced by Bill as "my sponsor, Ebby." At the dinner, Ebby did not appear to be a happy man, and his health was declining.

He had over seven months' sobriety and less than two years to live when he moved for the final time. And though he seemed to be an unlucky man who had lived under a cloud much of his life, he would find the silver lining and continuous sobriety in the end. His benefactor this time would be a loving, caring woman named Margaret McPike.

12

Peace at McPike's Farm

Ebby Thacher spent the last two years of his life in a pleasant farmhouse on a country road called Peaceable Street. The name was coincidental, but the outcome was the result of love and patience. Ebby did find a measure of peace there and an easing of the conflicts that had tormented him so much of his life.

The place was McPike's Farm, a pioneering alcoholism treatment facility in the town of Galway, near Saratoga Springs, New York. It lay only twenty-five miles north of Albany, Ebby's hometown. The mailing address for the farm is Ballston Spa, seven miles to the east. This was the address Bill Wilson always used in his reference to the home.

The rest home had been opened in the winter of 1958 by Margaret and Mickey McPike. Ebby, the resident best known to the AA community, arrived at the farm on May 30, 1964. He died in a hospital near there on March 21, 1966.

Fourteen years after Ebby's death and some time following the closing of McPike's Farm, Margaret still had a catch in her voice when she talked about the deep love she and Mickey felt for Ebby. They rightly saw him as a troubled man. His physical condition had deteriorated in the years since he had left Texas. Like Searcy W. and the other Texans, however, they

135

had accepted responsibility for Ebby as an assignment from Bill, and they never wavered.

"I was down in New York at a nursing convention, and Bill had called the Farm to see if we might take [Ebby], and Mickey told him I was in New York," Margaret said, recalling how the matter had first been proposed. She then went over to see Bill in his office at AA General Service. He asked her if she would take care of Ebby. Ebby was then at High Watch in Kent, Connecticut, but Bill thought he would do better with the McPikes. Margaret quickly agreed. They immediately made plans for Ebby's transfer.

Margaret and Mickey McPike with Bill Wilson (center)
on one of Bill's visits to the Farm to see Ebby.

In an interview several years later, Margaret was asked if Ebby was drunk when Bill drove him up to the Farm.

Oh, no, but he was very, very sick, and he was in bad physical condition. He had just refused to do anything for himself . . . he didn't want to take his medicine. He wouldn't do anything. And of course we had the doctor there and I spent Memorial Day with them. And Bill said that if [Ebby] needs anything more or if you feel it is too much for you to handle, let me know and I'll always be available.

So my doctor came, and he couldn't put him in a tub. His heart was not that good. But we did bed baths for about a week, and I always had some pretty good boys available. And I told him while he had a shower in his room, he should remember that he could get into the tub, or else the boys would do it for him, and if they don't I will.

The prospect of being forcibly bathed by Margaret apparently drove Ebby to agree to take the baths on his own.

═══════════════════════════════════════

The eleven-room farmhouse at McPike's Farm is currently the residence of Margaret's daughter, Margaret Donohue and her husband, Joe. It still attracts visitors who are interested in its long history as an alcoholic rest home. It was built in the first part of the nineteenth century and was more than a hundred years old when the McPikes launched it as a treatment facility. Located on five acres in a wooded rural setting, the house is a charming example of earlier New England home construction. It was a comfortable rest home but certainly not fancy or plush. The house has a slate roof. There is also an old red barn, with hand-hewn beams. Surrounding the property are horse chestnut and locust trees, with maple growth in the back and a stand of evergreens on an adjoining hill.

═══════════════════════════════════════

Margaret, who died early in 1982, related how Ebby had arrived at the farm in a miserable state of mind and then mellowed as the months passed under her care. She was a licensed practical nurse, but her more important qualification was in having a deep feeling for other people's suffering and a desire to help them. She handled Ebby gently, even in his depressed times, and he began to respond.

Until Ebby arrived at McPike's Farm, his life had not gone well following his return from Texas. While he had lived for a long time with the Wilsons, his stay with his brother Ken in Delmar, New York, may have ended badly. Ken's daughter, Ellen FitzPatrick, remembered that her parents had found more than thirty empty vodka bottles stashed about the house following Ebby's departure. This, and his declining health, made the future outlook for his well-being bleak.

Bill, always Ebby's attentive guardian and protector, discussed this in a 1964 letter to Olie L., the Texas member who had done so much for Ebby:

> Last winter I took [Ebby] over to Chit Chat Farms, where they have an excellent layout. This spring he spent a while at High Watch Farm—a drying out place near us that you have probably heard about. Just now he is at Margaret McPike's, a small farm setup near Schenectady. . . . He is not far from his brother Ken; also some of the Albany AA's. . . . However, he has scarcely the energy to talk to anyone.

Ebby had emphysema, the same illness that would afflict Bill in his final years. Both had been heavy smokers. Mary Lee J. mentioned Camels as Ebby's favorite cigarette. Bill himself never was able to stop smoking until the emphysema had all but overtaken him.

For the time being, Margaret has him in somewhat better physical condition. They have a good doctor in attendance, and there is a hospital devoted to lung troubles nearby. So this is the best that we can seem to do.

In this connection I recall with gratitude everything you and many AAs in Texas did in the days gone by to make Ebby better and happier than he had ever been before.

Though he was initially assigned a private room at McPike's Farm, the accommodations were arranged for dormitory-type living for seven men and five women. One large room had space for three men. Five women shared two rooms. The rustic dining table resembled the type used in parks for picnics, with built-in bench seats, and had been constructed of brown ash at a local sawmill.

The McPikes were so enthusiastic about Bill's visit and the confidence he had placed in them for Ebby's care that they insisted on having a picture taken on the day he arrived with Ebby. This was the first of many trips Bill would take to McPike's Farm, sometimes alone and at other times with Lois. Margaret and Mickey had a rule of never telling the other patients about one of Bill's planned visits until after he had arrived. Bill always chatted with the other patients, of course, and would sometimes take Ebby for a short drive through the beautiful countryside surrounding the Ballston Spa area. This is about 130 miles almost due north of the Wilsons' home in Bedford Hills, New York.

Margaret, who was fond of Bill, had first met him and Lois in 1951, at the dinner held for Bill every fall in New York City. She remembered that he and Lois had been married thirty-four years at the time.

In 1980, Margaret recalled that they kept Ebby in the private room for about a month after his arrival. An AA member named Harold S. cooked for the patients. He would prepare a breakfast tray to be sent up to Ebby. Even in the beginning and despite his condition, Ebby could finish a good breakfast, Margaret said. Then he was able to come down for lunch and would spend some time completing a crossword puzzle before doing some reading. Margaret recalled that Ebby was one of those rare individuals who could complete the *New York Times* crossword puzzle quickly. She said that he also had a good memory of things he wanted to remember, especially the people he'd had good times with. Margaret also thought that Ebby understood the AA program. Though some people considered him a weak person, Margaret thought he might have been exceptionally strong if not for his drinking.

McPike's farmhouse.

He never drank while at McPike's Farm, Margaret remembered. Beyond that, he never even tried to get a bottle, so the months before he went to the Farm and the entire time he stayed there were a long sober period. Though he never attended AA meetings, the atmosphere at the farm as well as the association with the McPikes and frequent visitors reflected the fellowship's outlook and purposes. It was fair to say, as his Texas sponsor Searcy W. has repeatedly stated, that Ebby was sober about 2½ years when he died.

In the beginning, Ebby might have felt that he would recover his health and then move elsewhere. He fitted in so well at McPike's Farm, however, that it became his home. Margaret recalled:

Ebby could feel at home because he knew he was well cared for and he was always with somebody. When he moved upstairs, he was never alone. I did have a special love for Ebby, through caring for him. I wanted to win his affection. Even though he'd be out of sorts and lose his temper, towards the end of the day he'd always say he was sorry.

But any temper outbursts must have been short-lived and not of the sort that put him at cross-purposes with others. The other patients at the farm always liked him, she explained, although he would talk little unless he really liked someone. He always liked the ladies, all of his life, she added with a smile.

What was Ebby's general outlook? "I think he was disappointed in his life," Margaret explained. She said he talked little about the first meeting with Bill that had eventually led to AA's founding. "He would talk more about people he had met, many of them celebrities," Margaret said. They could not get Ebby interested in playing cards or checkers. But he did like to reminisce and sometimes mentioned the airplane ride he'd taken with Bill in 1929 and the time he'd driven the car into a house and stepped out to ask for coffee.

Despite Ebby's poor physical condition, Margaret was never discouraged. "In caring for Ebby, and because he was so sick, the rewards of being a nurse is to see a patient become what we termed with Ebby—maximum of recovery, where he could dress himself and come down to meals twice a day," she said. "We had to help him dress." They helped Ebby with his bath, and Margaret sometimes gave him back rubs and trimmed his toenails. Ebby was also fond of Mickey, she said.

But while Ebby had found his safe home, his health was continuing to decline. On August 24, 1964, Bill wrote to George McQ. of Fort Worth, referring to his own recent Texas trip as "about the last of my traveling. And I had come to thank you Texans especially for what you had been doing for my own sponsor, Ebby." Bill, as with the Texas trip he had taken ten years earlier, made special mention of Ebby—a reason that explained his traveling to Texas while declining invitations to other localities.

He then brought George up to date on Ebby's situation:

> Since he got back up here, Ebby's emphysema has continued to catch up with him. He is really feeble now, scarcely able to walk 20 feet on the level without getting out of wind. He is now at McPike's Farm, R.D. 2, Ballston Spa, New York. Margaret McPike is a trained nurse and he is receiving nursing care for only $75 a week—a sum which he can make good out of his Social Security and financing of $200 a month that comes out of the AA book money at headquarters.
>
> Maybe some of you and the other boys would like to drop him a line—it would all help.

In January 1966, Ebby's brother Ken died in Albany. Ebby and Ken had been close in age. Ken, too, had had a drinking problem, according to his children. Unlike Ebby, however, Ken had a strong wife who had helped keep him afloat over the years. But Ken had been supportive of Ebby and, according to Searcy, had even gone to Texas once just to have the experience of seeing Ebby sober and well. Sadly, the doctor who attended Ebby's needs at the Farm felt that Ebby was too sick with a bad cold even to travel the twenty-five miles to Albany for Ken's funeral. Margaret did remember, however, that Ken's son, Ken, Jr., accompanied by his wife and young son, came to visit Ebby.

But Margaret did feel that Ebby seemed to give up after Ken died. Three months later, Eddie D., a former newspaperman who worked at Beech Hill, stopped by to visit McPike's Farm. He spent about an hour with Ebby. "It was just a general conversation," Eddie said, "one alcoholic to another. He looked real bad; there was a smell of death in the room."

The next day, the housekeeper at McPike's Farm told Margaret she thought Ebby was sick. Margaret went up to his room immediately. She recalled:

> I said, "Ebby, do you feel all right?" And he said, "No, I really don't." So I . . . checked his pulse and pressure, and I didn't like it. When I called the doctor, he told me that he didn't like the heart sounds. . . . He said [Ebby] might go into coronary failure any minute. . . .

Margaret, aided by the housekeeper, began to monitor Ebby's condition. At first Ebby resisted going to the hospital, but after Mickey came into his room and talked with him, he finally agreed. He began to talk as if he knew the end was near. He even ended with the remark, "Well, we all have to go sometime." Then, just after Mickey went downstairs to make a phone call, Ebby started to cough and Margaret removed his dentures. He collapsed back on the bed, and Margaret checked him with a stethoscope. "I couldn't get a radial pulse, but I got an apical. I think he had a slight cerebral," she recalled.

With Margaret holding his hand, Ebby was rushed to a nearby hospital in Ballston Spa. Over the weekend, he was still able to recognize Margaret. But by Sunday night he was comatose. He died at one in the morning. The cause of death was listed as cerebral thrombosis (stroke).

Bill and Lois were in Mexico but quickly returned for Ebby's wake and funeral, attended by a few friends and family members. The obituary in the newspaper was brief, noting that Ebby was a brother of the late Albany Mayor John Boyd Thacher II and had done clerical work in Texas and New York City. There was no mention of AA.

Ebby was laid to rest next to his brother Ken in the family plot in the Albany Rural Cemetery, just north of the city. In death, he rejoined his prominent family. The large monument that defines the Thacher plot is that of George H. Thacher, Ebby's distinguished grandfather and founder of the family firm. Ebby's parents and other relatives are also buried there.

In June, Bill's remembrance of Ebby was published in the *AA Grapevine*—a tribute that can be found today in *The Language of the Heart*. It expressed once again Bill's gratitude to Ebby for the long-ago act of sponsorship that had brought Bill to sobriety.

> Ebby had been enabled to bring me the gift of grace because he could reach me at depth through the language of the heart. He had pushed ajar that great gate through which all in AA have since passed to find their freedom under God.

Other friends mourned Ebby and recalled the key role he had in AA's founding. Few messages following Ebby's death were more touching than the letter sent to Mickey and Margaret McPike from a Texas group and personally signed by thirty-eight members: "We of the Highlands, Texas, group want to extend our warmest regard and to express our deep appreciation for the loving care you gave Ebby in the last years of his life. As you know he would be the last person who would want a lot of fanfare, praise, or belated recognition. The feeling that envelops the occupants of an AA Clubhouse nestled in the woods on the banks of the San Jacinto River . . . is best expressed by Edgar A. Guest." This was followed by a Guest poem titled "When Sorrow Comes."

After Ebby died, life went on at McPike's Farm. But Margaret and Mickey treasured their memories of him. New residents came and went, and Margaret continued to run the farm after Mickey's passing in 1971. Finally, in 1979, she knew it was time to retire, closed the center, and went to live with her daughter's family in Rotterdam Junction, New York. She passed away of an aneurysm at Boston's Deaconness Hospital on January 8, 1982.

Margaret McPike's outstanding work has been widely recognized, and the New York State Senate passed a special resolution in her honor shortly after her retirement. In 1986, almost five years after Margaret's death, the State of New York dedicated a new alcoholism treatment center in Utica to Margaret and Mickey McPike, honoring their achievements in helping alcoholics. The story accompanying the official news release stated that McPike's Farm had aided the recoveries of more than four thousand persons, including Ebby Thacher of Albany, who is credited with starting the recovery of Bill Wilson, the cofounder of Alcoholics Anonymous.

13

Ebby and the World of Relapse

The fellowship of Alcoholics Anonymous is like no other society in human experience. Its members agree at every meeting that they should share their experience, strength, and hope with each other, but their sharing of opinions is wild and unpredictable. Members can think and say almost anything they choose, the only guideline being that it be directed to the aim of staying sober. This, too, leaves considerable latitude, because so many things in a person's life involve problems related to sobriety.

But one belief is widely and firmly shared with an unshakable conviction: *Don't take a drink no matter what happens;* stay sober even if your world is falling apart! This belief is expressed in countless ways and is shared at every AA meeting. Quite often, in fact, an AA member will mention a particularly bad experience and then add, in a grateful tone, "At least I didn't drink over it!" Others at the table will nod approvingly at such a remark.

Continuous sobriety is so important that group membership lists often show the dates of each member's last drink. At large anniversary meetings, there are sometimes "countdowns" that reveal how long each member has been sober. A number of groups also issue "coins" that show the number of years a person has been sober. This practice may seem quaint or even tacky to people outside the fellowship, but it can carry deep meaning for AA members

Yet there have been many thousands of AA members who, like Ebby, have attained long periods of sobriety broken by periods of drinking, called slips in AA. Many of them, like Ebby, also helped others who went on to enjoy a lifetime of uninterrupted sobriety. Some of the AA pioneers whose stories appeared in the first edition of *Alcoholics Anonymous* were said to have had later troubles with alcohol; yet, their stories continued to help many.

How do we explain this, when at every meeting we say, from *Alcoholics Anonymous,* "Rarely does a person fall who thoroughly follows our path?" The answer is simple, because in

Ebby's illness was evident in his final months at McPike's Farm.

that same reading we also hear, "Remember that we deal with alcohol—cunning, baffling, powerful!" Alcoholics are indeed dealing with a cunning enemy, a baffling enemy, a powerful enemy. John Barleycorn, as alcohol used to be known, has many ways to trap the unwary alcoholic. We still don't know how to identify and expose all of the traps.

We'll never know of all the problems Ebby Thacher faced during the years between his first return to drinking in 1937 and his death in 1966. He had two years and seven months of continuous sobriety in the beginning, a long period of about seven years' sobriety in Texas in the 1950s, and about 2½ years' sobriety just before he died. Combined with shorter periods he was able to put together, he may have had fifteen years' sobriety during the thirty-two years following his initial contact with the Oxford Group. Since he was alcoholic, however, his drinking was destructive and always wiped out any personal gains he had made in sobriety.

We have stock answers to explain such patterns; one common explanation for such repeated slips is that the person "just isn't being honest." The AA explanation for such a problem, from *Alcoholics Anonymous,* is, "Those who do not recover are people who cannot or will not completely give themselves to this simple program, usually men and women who are constitutionally incapable of being honest with themselves."

If we apply this to a person such as Ebby, however, we find ourselves "taking his inventory," a practice that in itself is a violation of an AA principle! Just to say that the person "isn't honest" doesn't really explain why people continue on suicidal paths when they've had the opportunity as Ebby did, to learn so much about a better way of life.

It is also true that Ebby had a great deal of honesty in his personal makeup. Right at the beginning, when he was facing a court appearance, he could not sneak a few drinks of ale because he had promised the judge he would come back sober. He had to be honest with the judge, and in so doing he was also honest with himself and honest about his own motives.

This one act of honesty helped produce an attitude that kept him sober for well over two years. Most importantly, he was sober and dedicated during those critical weeks when he sponsored Bill, an action that led to AA's founding. Ebby had a wonderful feeling during that period, something he always remembered and sought to regain. Later on, in his repeated attempts to find and maintain sobriety, he was unable to recapture that same feeling or attitude. But why did he think such a feeling or attitude was even necessary for continuous sobriety? AA experience has at least taught us that alcoholics can stay sober even while going through periods of depression and disappointment.

We can also say that the recovering alcoholic, in Ebby's day and in our own, must swim against a tide of counteropinions in the general society. Alcohol is sometimes called "a drug of choice" because now an array of drugs is available that would have been hard to find in Ebby's day. It is still difficult to define alcoholism precisely. Every alcoholic must deal with the question, "Am I really an alcoholic or just a troubled person who was drinking a lot during a bad period in my life?" In Ebby's case, despite everything that happened, he still believed during the summer of 1954 that he might safely return to drinking. But when he tried it, the result was the same as in the past.

What causes such muddled thinking? It is always tempting to think that one's excessive drinking was caused by difficult conditions in personal circumstances, and that one will be able to drink moderately once these circumstances have improved. This view may have dominated past efforts by well-meaning professionals who attempted to treat alcoholics without understanding the absolute need to avoid the fatal first drink.

In today's troubled world, this muddled thinking continues because there are people who appeared to be alcoholics but have evidently learned to control their drinking. AA was not for them, and they resent having been prodded into the fellowship and exposed to a Twelve Step program they don't really like. This may occur at times because courts tend to require persons to attend AA meetings following a drink-related offense, such as driving while impaired. We cannot say that all such people are really alcoholics according to AA's view of the problem. These persons can say, with some justification, that they didn't really need AA when they continue to drink moderately without further trouble.

Ebby didn't face such examples, because court-mandated attendance at AA meetings wasn't on the scene in his day. He did have a tendency to be influenced by cronies and others whom he met during his travels. He could fit in with drinking crowds just as well as he sometimes fitted in with sober AA groups, depending on his needs at the time.

In our time, however, we do have examples of people who take exception to the emphasis AA puts on staying away from the first drink. When it doesn't work, the outcome can be extremely tragic. One tragedy of this kind was the death of Terry McGovern on December 13, 1994. Her death was publicized nationally because she was the daughter of George McGovern, a longtime U.S. Senator and the 1972 Democratic candidate for the U.S. presidency. Senator McGovern, shattered to the core by his daughter's death, reviewed her life and problems two years later in an excellent book, *Terry*, published by Villard Books.

Terry, like Ebby, had long periods of sobriety in AA, and one even lasted eight years. Senator McGovern detailed the almost superhuman efforts she had made to stay sober, and wrote:

I have tried to sort out that trail of recovery and relapse in her life. There is no certain explanation of why some alcoholics relapse and others do not. I know of no other alcoholic who devoted more time and effort to recovery than Terry. If she sometimes neglected regular participation in the AA program and then relapsed, this leaves unanswered the question of why she would drift away from AA in the first place, setting herself up for yet another relapse. Perhaps at some level, Terry was incapable of really saying farewell to her old but treacherous friend—alcohol.

While there are no complete explanations for such relapses, the bitter experience of those "who go back out" should convince any of us that we're on the right track in making an absolute out of staying away from the first drink. Others may feel that this is an exaggerated or extremist position, but they usually aren't down in the trenches with the people who see alcoholism for what it really is. Families like the McGoverns have seen the problem in all of its grim reality and can understand why a single drink—such a casual thing to the controlled drinker—is a deadly poison for the individual alcoholic.

We also know that these troubled persons who succumbed to the first drink may have done considerable good during their sober periods. They attended AA meetings, they sponsored others, they offered their own experience and hope at times when it was most needed. Indeed, Bill went out of his way, in *Alcoholics Anonymous Comes of Age,* to mention the example of Paddy, the Irishman who helped launch AA in Boston and hence in much of New England.

> The Boston group provided us with a fresh wonder and a big heartbreak, too. Its founder could never get sober himself and he finally died of alcoholism. Paddy was just too sick to make it. Slip followed slip, but he came back each

time to carry AA's message, at which he was amazingly successful. Time after time the group nursed him back to life.
Then came the last bender, and that was it. This very sick
man left behind him a great group and a triple-A rating for
valor.

Despite their contributions, those who relapse suffer pain and
troubles that nobody should have. Their troubles bring pain to
the people who love them. While we still don't have answers
for those caught in the world of relapse, we should make every
effort to support and encourage those who have fallen. Many
people make it back after having slips. We should continue to
hold these examples up for everyone to see. It is all right to ap-
plaud long-term sobriety, but we should give special applause
to the person who has trouble and is making it back into the
world of sobriety.

In his lifetime, Ebby had lots of help but also received lots
of criticism. We can learn from his example, and we can be
grateful that there were devoted AA members in several states
who went out of their way to help him.

Whatever troubles Ebby had, he carried the right message
to the right person at the right time. For that we should always
be grateful—to Ebby as well as to the Higher Power that set all
of this in motion.

Bibliography

AA World Services, Inc. *Alcoholics Anonymous*, 3d ed. New York: Alcoholics Anonymous World Services, Inc., 1976.

———. *Pass It On: The Story of Bill Wilson and How the AA Message Reached the World*. New York: Alcoholics Anonymous World Services, Inc., 1984.

———. *Alcoholics Anonymous Comes of Age: A Brief History of AA*. New York: Alcoholics Anonymous World Services, Inc., 1985.

Bigelow, Edwin L., and Nancy H. Otis. *Manchester, Vermont, 1761–1961: A Pleasant Land Among the Mountains*. Manchester, VT: Rod and Reel Publishing, 1981. (Originally published 1961 by the Town of Manchester.)

James, William. *The Varieties of Religious Experience*. New York: Collier, 1961.

Kennedy, William. *O Albany!: Improbable City of Political Wizards, Fearless Ethnics, Spectacular Aristocrats, Splendid Nobodies, and Underrated Scoundrels*. New York: Penguin, 1985.

McGovern, George S. *Terry: My Daughter's Life-and-Death Struggle with Alcoholism*. New York: Villard, 1996.

Wilson, Bill. *The Language of the Heart*. New York: AA Grapevine, 1988.

Wilson, Lois. *Lois Remembers: Memoirs of the Co-Founder of Al-Anon and Wife of the Co-Founder of Alcoholics Anonymous*. New York: Al-Anon Family Group Headquarters, 1979.

About the Author

Mel B., a recovering alcoholic, has written numerous articles and essays on the subject of Twelve Step programs. He is a retired business writer and has lived in Toledo, Ohio, since 1972. As a free-lance writer, he contributes regularly to *Business Venture,* a regional publication, and Toledo's daily newspaper, *The Blade.* He is also a contributor to *Mature Living,* a Toledo-area paper for senior citizens. Born in Norfolk, Nebraska, he served in the U.S. Navy in the Pacific during World War II and lived for many years in Jackson, Michigan. He and his wife Lori, a retired fashion illustrator, have four grown children and six grandchildren.

Mel B. has authored pamphlets for Hazelden including *Pride, Step 10: Maintaining My New Life,* and *Step 11: Partnership With a Higher Power.* His other Hazelden books are *New Wine* (1991) and *Walk in Dry Places* (1996).

About Hazelden Publishing

As part of the Hazelden Betty Ford Foundation, Hazelden Publishing offers both cutting-edge educational resources and inspirational books. Our print and digital works help guide individuals in treatment and recovery, and their loved ones. Professionals who work to prevent and treat addiction also turn to Hazelden Publishing for evidence-based curricula, digital content solutions, and videos for use in schools, treatment programs, correctional programs, and electronic health records systems. We also offer training for implementation of our curricula.

Through published and digital works, Hazelden Publishing extends the reach of healing and hope to individuals, families, and communities affected by addiction and related issues.

For more information about Hazelden publications,
please call **800-328-9000**
or visit us online at **hazelden.org/bookstore.**